SELECTED POEMS AND ESSAYS

Alice Meynell (née Thompson) was born in Barnes, Surrey (now London), in 1847 to a middle-class family of artistic and intellectual inclinations. She and her sister Elizabeth, later Lady Butler, a celebrated historical painter, were brought up in somewhat Bohemian style in various locations, including Liguria and the Isle of Wight. In 1868 Alice converted to Roman Catholicism and at around the same time fell in love with Father Dignam, the priest who received her into the Church. This impossible love informed many of her early poems. Her first volume of verse, *Preludes*, was published by Henry S. King in 1875 with illustrations by her sister. In the following year she met Wilfrid Meynell, a young journalist and fellow Catholic convert who admired her poems, and they married in 1877. (The name is pronounced to rhyme with 'fennel'.) The Meynells worked both jointly and independently on journalistic work, co-editing and copywriting for several periodicals as well as writing literary and critical essays, signed and unsigned, for others. They became important figures in the London literary world. Approached by the Catholic poet Francis Thompson, a homeless opium-addict seeking publication, they published and promoted his work and supported him financially and morally for the rest of his life. They had eight children, of whom one died in infancy. Several of the Meynell children became involved in literary life.

Alice Meynell became established as a prolific and highly respected essayist, especially from the 1890s when her work began to be collected into books. The republication early in that decade of her youthful poems, along with a small number of more recent ones, also raised her reputation, and in later life she returned to more frequent writing in verse. Her books of essays and poems, published at first mainly by John Lane at The Bodley Head and from 1913 by Burns and Oates, were many times reprinted, and she was in high demand as a columnist and reviewer. An outspoken advocate for women's suffrage as well as other political causes, she was President of the Society of Women Journalists and Vice-President of the Women Writers' Suffrage League. On two occasions she was proposed for the role of Poet Laureate. She inspired ardent and devoted friendships, notably in the poet Coventry Patmore (whose passionate love for her necessitated a painful break in their friendship) and in George Meredith during his final years. In 1911 the Meynell family moved to Greatham, Sussex. Alice Meynell died in 1922 at the age of seventy-five.

Alex Wong is the author of two collections of poetry, *Poems Without Irony* (2016) and *Shadow and Refrain* (2021). His original and translated verse has appeared widely, as have his critical essays on English literature. He is the author of a critical book, *The Poetry of Kissing in Early Modern Europe* (2017), and has taught for over a decade at the University of Cambridge. For Carcanet he has previously edited and introduced the works of A.C. Swinburne and Walter Pater.

Laura Mulvey is Professor of Film, Emerita, at Birkbeck College, University of London. She is the author of *Visual and Other Pleasures* (1989/2009), *Fetishism and Curiosity* (1996/2013), *Citizen Kane* (1992/2012), *Death Twenty-four Times a Second: Stillness and the Moving Image* (2006) and *Afterimages: On Cinema, Women and Changing Times* (2019). She made six films in collaboration with Peter Wollen, including *Riddles of the Sphinx* (1977) and *Frida Kahlo and Tina Modotti* (1980). With artist/filmmaker Mark Lewis, she has made *Disgraced Monuments* (1994) and *23 August 2008* (2013).

Alice Meynell

edited by Alex Wong

Selected Poems and Essays

with a preface by Laura Mulvey

CARCANET CLASSICS

First published in Great Britain in 2025 by
Carcanet
Main Library, The University of Manchester
Oxford Road, Manchester, M13 9PP
www.carcanet.co.uk

A CIP catalogue record for this book is
available from the British Library.

ISBN 978 1 80017 501 3

Book design by Andrew Latimer, Carcanet
Typesetting by LiteBook Prepress Services
Printed in Great Britain by SRP Ltd, Exeter, Devon

The publisher acknowledges financial
assistance from Arts Council England.

CONTENTS

ESSAYS

PREFACE

I am very grateful to Alex Wong for inviting me to write a Preface to his anthology of poems and essays by my great-grandmother, Alice Meynell. His selection, particularly of her essays, has definitely strengthened my earlier, rather guarded, sense of the relevance of the term 'feminism' for her work. He points out that 'she uses the new-coined word herself, with wary quotation marks, though not disowning its meaning'. Alice Meynell wrote about male writers and cultural figures and her perspective is not consistently 'woman-orientated'. However, concentrating on her prose writing for this Preface, I've found the originality and radicality of her ideas striking. On the one hand, her feminism is overt. She denounced male misogyny (as forcefully illustrated by several of the essays in this selection) and she wrote over and over again about women's achievements, whether recognised or insufficiently recognised by conventional history and culture. On the other hand, her feminism more subtly, but inextricably, inflects her choice of topics, her modes of thought and how she translates those thoughts into words.

Although A.M. was only occasionally a poet, she was a professional journalist.[1] She and her husband, Wilfrid Meynell, produced two short-lived literary journals during the 1880s, and from 1881 to 1900 they also collaborated in the constant struggle to produce the *Weekly Register* (a Catholic periodical), Wilfrid's bread and butter. A.M. embarked on her

---

1 I have been unsure how to name my great-grandmother in this Preface. She was always known to her grandchildren and beyond as 'Gammer' (Wilfrid was 'Gaffer'), and then, more formally, as 'A.M'. I have great difficulty with the academically acceptable 'Meynell', which feels too alien and forced, due to our relationship. I have alternated between 'Alice Meynell' and 'A.M'., my preference.

intense essay-writing career in 1889, after six of her children were born (one had died in infancy and two were still to come). Her essays were all commissioned by various journals that flourished in the late nineteenth century. Her weekly contribution to the *Pall Mall Gazette* column 'The Wares of Autolycus' drew immediate critical and reader acclaim and attention, leading to subsequent essay collections published by John Lane and others. She worked hard, sometimes owing 16,000 words a week. Family legend has it that she wrote all morning in the sacrosanct space of her room, only emerging for lunch and to join the hectic, deadline-driven chaos at the library table in 47 Palace Court, Bayswater.

Alex astutely characterises the structure of Alice Meynell's essays as 'connective': a progression that moves surprisingly but naturally from one idea or observation to another. But, I thought, might a mixture of looseness and surprising turnings be relevant both to the essay form and to women's writing? I remembered a remark of Elizabeth Hardwick's: 'We would not want to think of the essay as the country of old men, but it is doubtful that the slithery form, wearisomely vague and as chancy as trying to catch a fish in the open hand, can be taught'. Perhaps, it seemed to me, this unregulated, undefined 'country' might offer women writers a literary 'room of their own'.[2] I also remembered Theodor Adorno's polemical defence of the essay as a form that challenged and evaded the rigidities of logic and reason—spheres of intellectual activity, incidentally, that had traditionally been closed to women. He says:

> Concepts do not form a continuum of operations. Thought does not progress in a single direction; instead the moments are interwoven as in a carpet.

---

2 Hardwick, 'Its Only Defense: Intelligence and Sparkle', in the *New York Times* (14 Sept 1986).

The fruitfulness of the thought depends on the density of the texture [...]. The essay proceeds methodically un-methodically.[3]

Although A.M. exploits the form's freedoms, she often ends with a specific, quite intense, thought, sometimes illuminating, sometimes perplexing, that leaves the reader pondering.

'The Rhythm of Life', the first essay in this selection, offers a case in point. The topic is time, which, A.M. suggests in the first sentence, is 'metrical'. In this visualisation of temporality as non-linear, I recognised an early form of today's feminists' aversion to linear time, to its associations with a patriarchally conceived history and chronologically compiled achievements. Here she argues in prose for a concept of time that often recurs in her poetry: leaping backwards and forwards, bringing past and future into dialogue. Oliver Hawkins has pointed out, for instance, that in A.M.'s early poem, 'A Letter from a Girl to her Own Old Age', time is criss-crossed—'before cinema had taught us to understand flash-backs and fast-forwards'.[4] Meanwhile the idea of 'recurrence' in 'The Rhythm of Life' evokes for me, as someone influenced by psychoanalytic theory, the unconscious mind, outside logical order and sequence, the source of non-sequitur thoughts and actions. In both instances, time is fluid.

But the essay's argument moves on, apparently at a tangent, to the particular 'rhythm of life' that's derived from the moon. The moon is given a feminine article: 'her metrical phases' are the source of her natural and cultural power, and she is subject to 'the order of recurrence'. Although a more explicit

3   Adorno, 'The Essay as Form', in *Notes to Literature*, ed. Rolf Tiedemann, vol. 1 (1991), p. 13.

4   Oliver Hawkins, a great-grandson of Alice Meynell, from an unpublished paper, 'Against the Flight of Time'.

association between femininity and cyclical time is not made, it's sufficiently implied for any reader, as I did, to recognise and reflect on further. These 'cumulative' thoughts, to my mind at least, hint, as nearly as might be possible at the end of the nineteenth century, at the 'periodicity' of menstruation. The essay then returns to the general problem of the need in life to 'do away with the hope and fear of continuance'. Its final sentence ends with a surprising, unresolved, juxtaposition, leaving the reader puzzling, trying to decipher what the writer might mean by 'the law that rules all things—a sun's revolutions and the rhythmic pangs of maternity'.

While 'A Woman in Grey' is written with Alice Meynell's characteristic loose connectivity, it also has a more unusual, symmetrical pattern, opening and closing with two quotations from Shakespeare, both evoking the strong influence of a mother on a son. This tighter structure gives special weight to the essay's central section, but it's prefaced, slightly blurring the symmetry, with some acute and extremely important points about gender binaries: the social tradition that imposes stasis on women while their male equivalents enjoy unfettered freedom of movement. If, as the essay points out, the battle of Waterloo was won 'on the playing fields of Eton', there was some other place 'where the future wives of the football players were sitting still'. Here the essay speaks the unspoken side of the movement/stillness opposition, naming the unmentioned feminine that heroic masculinity depends on but obscures.

A specific moment, observed in real life, turns the traditional opposition upside down. A.M., travelling on a bus along Oxford Street, notices a woman in grey riding a bicycle calmly through the chaos of the traffic churning all around her: through 'omnibuses and carriages, cabs and carts'. 'Beside all the unequal movement, there were the stoppings. It was a delicate tangle to keep from knotting'. The woman moves with a 'watchful confidence' and 'unstable equilibrium', passing between security and danger: 'she leapt into a life of moments. No pause was possible to her as she went except the vibrating pause of a perpetual change and an unflagging flight'. A.M.'s prose style vividly conjures up the scene's double temporality: its instantaneity, as she had observed it, and then, as she interprets it, its break with past precedent. Here the essay deviates from conventional linguistic transparency. Although, on a literal level, the simultaneity of 'pause' and 'perpetual change' might relate to the way a bicycle works, on a more figurative level there's a suggestion of paradox, even a confusion of logical sequence. The added adjectives, 'vibrating' and 'perpetual', then further disturb their nouns: the quiet of 'pause' is physically shaken and the prospect of 'change' has no end in sight. A.M. not only captures this hitherto unimaginable insertion of a female presence in, and movement through, the mass of 'male-dominated' traffic, but she also dissolves traditional binaries in the seeming contradiction of 'unstable equilibrium'.

The essay moves: from the actual bicyclist to her subversive significance as a woman in motion, and then to her wider allegorical associations. 'She evidently had not in her mind a single phrase, familiar to women, made to express no confidence except in accidents [...]. No woman could ride a bicycle along Oxford Street with that kind of baggage about her'. Here the bicyclist acquires implications beyond herself: she stands for the way the female psyche had been, and must continue to be, reconfigured in order for mobility to displace stasis. Furthermore, in the same spirit, in her progression along Oxford Street, the bicyclist represents the Movement, the on-going struggle for Women's Rights, the politics of progress with which Alice Meynell so deeply identified.

Alex's selection of A.M.'s essays concludes with four that, although not 'women-related', have a special significance for her idiosyncratic writing style as well as her way of seeing and relating to the world. These essays all revolve around her intense pleasure in natural phenomena; most particularly, perceptions and sensations produced by their movement and transience. This 'Alice Meynell' counters the image that so often haunts her: of austerity, reserve, reticence, withdrawal, etc. On the contrary, she writes as passionately about a passing cloud as she does about the rights of women. For the reader, these essays can transform old, habitual ways of seeing into unforgettable lessons in looking.

Due, perhaps, to my interest in the photographic image (still or moving), I've been struck by A.M.'s ability to capture immediacy in her prose. In certain passages, an original moment seems to leave its trace in her writing, printed, as it were, into the print on the page—just as light leaves an imprint on photosensitive paper. For André Bazin, a photograph is a natural phenomenon, untouched by the hand of man. In an interestingly analogous sleight of the imagination, the natural phenomena celebrated in these essays are all indifferent to, only rarely affected by, human presence. A.M. loved certain landscape painters (see, for instance, her thoughts on Corot's early morning light in the essay on the 'Hours of Sleep', included here). But on a different aesthetic register, simplicity defined nature's fascinating affects, precisely due to a lack of mediation, and the absence of ingenuity. For instance, in her essay 'Ceres' Runaway' (collected into a 1909 volume of the same title) she celebrates wildflowers growing high in Rome's ancient ruins. And this aesthetic of simplicity extends further. For instance, in an essay on the Brontës:

> The student passes delighted through the several courtyards of poetry, from the outer to the inner, from riches to more imaginative riches, and from decoration to more complex decoration; and prepares himself for the greater opulence of the innermost chamber. But when he crosses the last threshold

he finds this midmost sanctuary to be a hypaethral temple, and in its custody and care a simple earth and a space of sky.[5]

The essays on 'Cloud', 'Shadows', 'Horizon' and 'Reflections' observe the beauty of simplicity and of chance. Only in 'Horizon' is human experience necessary to create movement, the sensation of being raised up through and into a series of constantly shifting views, from a small dell to a distant seascape. She attributes a kind of autonomy to the natural forces that spread their beauty onto the world: the transient and insubstantial immediacy of light, for example, in clouds or on water, when set in motion by the wind. Clouds control light, 'distributing the sun' and decorating the earth, while their statuesque shapes decorate the sky. The shadow 'rushes to meet its bird when the bird swoops on to a branch and clings'. A.M.'s prose captures the complexity of these natural phenomena: 'shade and shine have been entangled as though by some wild wind through their million molecules'. And 'Reflections' pictures the visuality and physicality, then the instability, of a reflection on water: 'it is shattered to bits, it is flung wide, it is intricate with fine shadows'. Throughout the essays, A.M. bemoans London, lost under the fog, until at the very end of 'Reflections', suddenly 'a thousand replies to the sunset shine in the windows of the streets'.

It's quite usual to consider Alice Meynell's childhood, and most especially the influence of her father, Thomas Thompson, in any assessment of her character and her literary work. However, her original way of observing the world around

---

5 'Charlotte and Emily Brontë', in *Essays of To-day and Yesterday*, ed. Wilfrid Meynell (1925), pp. 44-57; pp. 53-54. Thanks to Mark Dallyn, A.M.'s great-grandson, for giving me a copy of this very special collection of her essays on women writers, and for pointing out this passage to me.

her, as well as her extraordinary responsiveness to natural beauty, come from her mother, Christiana. Alice and her older sister, Elizabeth (who grew up to be an eminent painter), were educated by their father, whose outstanding erudition, intellectual precision and devotion to literature were undoubtedly absorbed and emulated by his literary daughter. Vita Sackville-West, in her otherwise perceptive Introduction to the centenary publication of A.M.'s *Prose and Poetry* (1947), sets up a dichotomy between the parents. She says: 'It is easy to trace the influence of [her father's] austerity upon the spirit that later informed every gesture of Alice Meynell'. On the other hand, her mother is described as 'a somewhat feckless, ecstatic, sentimental, "artistic", example of Victorian womanhood'.[6]

Charles Dickens, Christiana's former admirer and Thompson's one-time best friend, gives an illuminating account of an 1853 visit to the Thompsons' 'beautiful situation in a ruinous palace' near Genoa. Dickens says: 'We had disturbed [Christiana] at her painting in oils, and I have rather received the impression that, what with that, and what with music, the household affairs went a little to the wall'. He found Thompson teaching 'the little girls multiplication tables in a disorderly old billiard room'.[7] To my mind, Elizabeth and Alice were saved from any correct womanly preparation for domestic life and its duties by the combined influence of both parents: the education, rigorous, if eccentric, they received from their father and their mother's complete indifference to housekeeping in favour of her art. (It would be quite often noted in later years that women's traditional skills were not Mrs. Meynell's *forte*.)

---

6 Sackville-West, 'Introduction', in Alice Meynell, *Prose and Poetry: Centenary Volume* (1947), p. 11, p. 10.

7 Viola Meynell, *Alice Meynell: A Memoir* (1929), p. 17.

Christiana Weller had been a successful concert pianist when she married Tom Thompson in 1845, bringing her promising professional career to an end. From 1851, they spent half of every year in Italy, where Christiana began to paint. Her diaries record her responses to the varying lights and colours of land, sky and sea, their changeability and their transience and her constant striving to capture these effects in their elusive moments of perfection. Her grand-daughter, Viola Meynell, in her *Memoir* of her mother (Alice), describes the diary entries as 'flying impressions': 'They telegraph themselves onto the page as if they were recorded in the actual hurry of their happening, instead of the quiet pause afterwards'.[8]

Christiana's diary entries do, indeed, tend towards the 'ecstatic', as she records her vivid visual impressions and emotions swaying, as Viola puts it, from rapture to distress. For instance, after the distress of a cold, difficult journey, rapture: 'Sun shone sweetly and three large trees on the opposite side of the *Place* made waving shadows on the walls'. Or, when in Italy: 'Magical morn. No white paint. Despair'.[9] To reiterate: Alice Meynell learnt lessons in looking from her mother, not only her passion for natural beauty but also her unusual responsiveness to everyday life; Christiana's ability, that is, to transform the otherwise ordinary into the extraordinary, into event and anecdote. In 'the quiet pause afterwards', the daughter's own observations of the everyday telegraphed the 'hurry of things happening' onto her pages.

The characterisation of Alice Meynell as 'austere' overlooks the way that emotion, or feeling, acts as a driving force within many of her essays. This is perhaps most obvious in her observations of childhood and her close identification

---

8 *Ibid.*, p. 14.
9 *Ibid.*, p. 21.

with children (see, in this selection, 'The Child of Tumult', 'The Child of Subsiding Tumult' and 'Near the Ground'), but it's evident too in her fascination with the natural world. It's also there in her response to 'A Woman in Grey'. But emotion is subjected, first, to a rigorous process of thought and then refracted into A.M.'s highly controlled literary style. There are moments when her writing gives the reader pause for thought. Sometimes these moments seem to me to prefigure a modernist rejection of writing for easy habits of reading (a 'making strange'). Or, I wonder, do they prefigure Hélène Cixous's concept (in her 1975 essay 'The Laugh of Medusa') of 'écriture feminine', women's errant, anti-patriarchal mode of writing?

In the Introduction to this selection, Alex has given a fascinating analysis of Alice Meynell's sense of a 'wildness' within herself, which she acknowledged while always also searching for its regulation.

> In the tension between wildness and law, according to the conceit of that late poem ['The Laws of Verse'], instead of a drifting feather she can be a bird in flight, with the bird's weight, its will, its orderly wingbeat, and the freedom and propulsion these allow. The bird she chooses in that poem is the skylark, famously free in song as well as in motion.

The transition from feather to bird presents a particular challenge to women writers: how to acquire 'weight' and 'wingbeat' without succumbing to a law which is not only not theirs, but also enforces their silence? This dilemma has preoccupied those contemporary feminists who have argued that the Freudian/Lacanian theory of the Oedipus complex gives a compelling account of the origins and perpetual renewal of women's oppression. To sum up the patriarchal pattern: when a child learns the rules of language, it exchanges bodily dependence on its mother for the society, culture, etc., that is ruled by the law of the Father, his 'Symbolic Order'. Women's potential for thought and creativity, silenced in this divided world, might turn to this 'wildness' in opposition to Law. But, in the process of the feather's transition to bird, as an acultural wildness finds its own voice, perhaps a different, alternative, Symbolic begins to be born.

Imposing contemporary feminist thought on a writer working over a century ago might well risk anachronism. But, to my mind, Alice Meynell's writing, her version of an *'écriture feminine'*, consciously breaks boundaries to depict, vividly, new ways of experiencing the world. For instance, 'The Rhythm of Life' turns upside down a traditional idea of time: 'recurrence' undermines the age-old image of an aspirational and one-dimensional future. And then: 'A Woman in Grey' witnesses nothing less than a reconfiguration of the female psyche, leaping forward into freedom, and casting the oppression of traditional stillness aside. This is not to suggest that (in either form or content) she stands for an essentially feminine aesthetic or worldview. Rather, A.M. contributes to a *woman-inflected* perspective. Her voice and her insights work to re-balance a culture that had been deprived, for so long, of fifty *per cent* of its creative potential.

A last, personal note. My generation of great-grandchildren grew up without knowing A.M. (she died in 1922) but with an acute awareness of her. Our immediate family tree is traced back to W. and A.M. and the family still meets at Greatham, the country home they acquired in 1911. A.M. has always been greatly admired for achieving acclaim in a male-dominated literary world and for her fervent support for women's rights. But writing this Preface, I've found, if late in life, a new sense of affinity with my great-grandmother. My writing, going back to the 1970s, has been rooted in feminist-influenced ways of thought, but it has, also, always been essayistic. It's probably due to A.M.'s aura, as a pioneering woman intellectual, that her female descendants have been unusually intellectually encouraged and valued. I benefited fully from this legacy as I grew up. And as, by some fortunate chance, I inherited my great-grandmother's writing table, I can imagine that I have, at least to some extent, written in her footsteps.

Laura Mulvey
2025

INTRODUCTION

Alice Meynell (1847–1922) was a major English author of the last quarter of the nineteenth century and the opening decades of the twentieth. The evidence of this is not to be found only in the manifest value of her writing itself, though this ought to be the more important thing. She was admired, celebrated and almost venerated by some of the most serious-minded of her peers, and meanwhile popular enough to attract large and enthusiastic audiences on extended lecture tours in the United States. If Coventry Patmore's personal devotion to her casts doubt on his impartiality in calling her prose 'the finest that was ever written',[1] strong praise of both her prose and her verse is easy to find in plenty from other quarters. Her journalistic work, editorial as well as authorial, was energetic, prolific, various and far-reaching, and her essays and criticism maintained the highest literary standards amid the rush, ephemerality and financial imperatives of periodical publishing. She was President of the Society of Women Journalists and Vice-President of the Women Writers' Suffrage League. As a poet, she was a serious contender (not that she herself contended) for the laureateship on two occasions. Passages of even her earliest poetry, which she herself came to deprecate, were called by Ruskin 'the finest things I've seen or felt in modern verse'.[2]

Meynell is a writer full of surprises, ones that justify themselves by their serious imaginative thoughtfulness: not flights of fancy, though she could respond to these, but imagination dedicated to realities as she saw them. 'The surprise coming on us', George Meredith said of her essays,

---

1   Quoted in Viola Meynell, *Alice Meynell: A Memoir* (1929), p. 120.

2   *Ibid.*, pp. 51-52; quoted also in June Badeni, *The Slender Tree: A Life of Alice Meynell* (1981), p. 52.

'from their combined grace of manner and sanity of thought is like one's dream of what the recognition of a new truth would be'.[3] Within chosen bounds of form and style—bounds she was always ready to acknowledge and emphasise, and which, in her verse especially, belonged to standards already somewhat classical—she found an authentic distinctiveness and an enabling space from which, with acuity, moral courage and wit, she could challenge routine expectations.

In a late poem, 'The Laws of Verse', which closes the selection of poems in this anthology, she writes about these bounds that contain, and yet somehow enable, a wildness inside. In poetry, as in other areas of life, that inner wildness could flourish and be turned to good account within the safety of the outer laws, and she submitted to literary laws as well as to the moral doctrine of her religion (she was a Catholic convert) with a conviction that these, in curtailing some freedoms, were conditions of a freedom more worthwhile. The poem invokes the 'laws' of verse, of versification, which are to meet around her like embracing arms: she is not only 'ruled' by them but also 'warmed'. Held by these laws, she becomes newly 'aware'—of her own breath and rhythm, the fundamentals of voice—and can 'feel her wild heart beat'. I think she believed that an unheld wildness, the wild heart left only to its wildness, could be random, indulgent, destructive, and would lack a creative tension, but that with discipline it could find its creativeness and self-insight. At any rate the wild heart was a human truth to be honoured it its place, and the 'wild' was one of the things she sought in poetry. 'The nearest she could get to defining the poetry she loved best', Viola Meynell wrote of her mother, 'was to say that it had the quality of wildness'.[4]

---

3 'Mrs. Meynell's Two Books of Essays', *National Review* 27:162 (Aug 1896), 762-70; p. 762. Quoted in *Alice Meynell*, p. 132.

4 *Alice Meynell*, p. 202.

In the tension between wildness and law, according to the conceit of that late poem, instead of a drifting feather she can be a bird in flight—with the bird's weight, its will, its orderly wingbeat, and the freedom and propulsion these allow. The bird she chooses in that poem is the skylark, famously free in song as well as in motion.

Out of this constant tension she administered her surprises. Conscience seems to have occupied the place of a muse to her, and often the surprises, paradoxes and second thoughts are those of an active self-examination, while at other times, more generally, the striking phrase or image is licensed and guaranteed by the artistic, moral and intellectual conscientiousness of an unsentimental and painstaking mind. 'Mrs. Meynell is always to be trusted', said Vita Sackville-West, who introduced the last anthology of Meynell's verse and prose—as long ago as 1947.[5]

(i) Style and Thought

'November Blue' begins as a poem lamenting the lack of blue sky in modern London, where metropolitan pollution does away with that 'heavenly colour' even in the narrow gaps between buildings where, for the hemmed-in Londoner, the sky is parcelled up into modest slivers. Another poet of the period might have continued in the same vein, ending the poem in dismay, or drawing out a sobering moral or spiritual lesson in the manner of Ruskin. Still another would have made a deliberately 'decadent' virtue of the smog, with lurid imagery and an attitude of knowingly morbid or perverse delight in the effects of urban contamination. What Alice Meynell does in the second half of her poem is to tread her own path,

---

5   Alice Meynell, *Prose and Poetry: Centenary Volume* (1947), p. 18.

offering the reader a sharply focused observation, vividly and imaginatively expressed, and combining the spiritual implication of the one approach (though free from righteous judgement) with the other's openness to strange modern beauty (though untouched by morbidity). It makes one wish one could see the effect it describes: the blue glow of a damp November evening by gaslight in fin-de-siècle London. This is not the natural blue of the sky but an accident of artificial life. And yet it is blue all the same—the heavenly colour, which 'comes to earth' and 'walks the streets'. For those who will take it, there is a religious suggestion there in addition to the brilliant poetry of description and appreciation, and I think it would be wrong to see one element as merely a vehicle or opportunity for the other. The connection for the poet is not an arbitrary one, a trick of rhetoric, but somehow a real one.

Her habit was a hard one—of resisting habit. 'November Blue' offers a good illustration of Meynell's preference for refreshed thinking and her reluctance to fall in too readily with comfortable grooves of thought.

Similarly characteristic, and likewise declining to come to rest in its first, more predictable thought, is her poem 'The Threshing-Machine'. Rather late to be quite topical, it is about the replacement of age-old manual threshing—a communal ritual of the harvest, often accompanied by songs in time with its human rhythms—by efficient but unpoetical machines. Behind the theme is all the controversy, unease and political debate of the preceding century over industrialisation and mechanisation, with a recognition of the continuing importance for nature and society of the larger tide of change. 'No "fan is in his hand" for these / Young villagers beneath the trees, / Watching the wheels', she begins. The opening reference is to Matthew 3:11-12:

… he that cometh after me is mightier than I, whose shoes I am not worthy to bear: he shall baptize you with the Holy Ghost, and with fire: Whose fan is in his hand, and he will throughly purge his floor, and gather his wheat into the garner; but he will burn up the chaff with unquenchable fire.

The poem regrets the loss of the Christian symbolism of the winnowing, the wheat and the chaff: 'all their symbols evermore / Forgone in England now'. The 'visible pledge' of that scriptural metaphor would no longer be visible as a real part of the business of life. For the poet who could make the play of smog and lamplight into a visible pledge or symbol of the Incarnation, this must have been a consideration of some weight, not simply an opportunity for a serviceable poetical thought. Her nostalgic yearning for Italy, which is most likely where she had seen manual winnowers at work in her expatriate childhood, also perhaps makes an element of the general nostalgia here.

But the nostalgia, sincere as it must be, gives way, as in 'November Blue', to a surprising new note. She gets there by way of a stanza of arch meditation and deft rhythmic modulation—almost too deft, or too pat, except that this seems to be part of the game (stanza 3). Tonally wrongfooting, these lines nevertheless convey a meaning that is never taken back, although they terminate with a sharp turn: 'And did our Ruskin speak too soon?'

A resonant voice against the sweep of mechanisation in modern capitalistic enterprises, Ruskin had told audiences of a lecture in 1883: 'all noble motion is with the limbs God has balanced for you, and all noble strength with the arms He has knit'. Human strength 'unaided' by machines was still the only 'divine strength', and he called this 'the strength of Herakles'.[6] Meynell's feelings in front of the threshing-machine send her back to this passage, with which she cannot agree. 'As the wheels ran', she says, 'I saw the other strength of man, / I knew the brain of Hercules'. Although there is a touch of irony in the sly transition from the first thought to the second, the poem is scrupulously fair and respectful and does not take sarcastic aim at Ruskin (about whom Meynell had written an appreciative and nuanced book in 1900). Along with him she feels the loss, but she has her own counter-thought to add. The poem does not pull down a prior view of things: it stands within it and finds something else worth saying; it adds balance and leaves the matter a complex one.

Meynell's lyrics are frequently formed from a single, more or less complex conceit, with everything subordinated to that one thought. They do not always, however, make the sort of sharp mental turn we have just seen. Sometimes the balance is indicated from the outset. 'The Lady Poverty' belongs to this class, a poem that contrasts the medieval Catholic ideal of holy poverty, the simple existence exemplified by such saints as Francis and Clare, with the hard and degrading realities of poverty in her own modern society. She does not do away with the old ideal, but will not indulge the facile sentimentality of the comfortable by misapplying it in a context it cannot fit. Less dramatically surprising, a poem like this—or an essay—is equally challenging and complex.

The thought that forms the kernel of an Alice Meynell poem is often of a paradoxical kind. 'Parentage', a strange and memorable poem—one that troubled Meredith, her great literary confidant of the time, with its unexpected note of fatalism—is one of these. The epigraph refers us to the original stimulus for its thought. Any notion that this is a dry piece of

---

6   *The Art of England*, lecture 4, ¶ 118.

cleverness for its own sake must be dispelled by the peculiar poignancy of the final line, which comes as the delayed passionate utterance that the rest of the poem—with its patches of grandiloquence, its Latinate polysyllables, its grand imagery, alliterations, the high style of its ostentatiously well-arrayed syntax—had somehow been hiding or postponing. The last line, made of simple monosyllabic words, free of Latinity, with the simpler, more naïve rhetoric of its final repetition, carries the emotion of something more than a love of paradox. Is there a note here of that powerful conviction of death she attributes to the poetry of the sixteenth century, and *not* to the writing of her own time, in her subtle essay 'The Lady of the Lyrics'?

Delighting in serious wit and counterintuitive insight, sometimes Meynell shows the influence of the seventeenth-century English poets she loved, though of course with great differences in diction and tone. 'To the Body' has its Metaphysical qualities, as do the eucharistic images of both 'A General Communion' and 'In Portugal, 1912'. A poem in which she felt particular pride, 'The Two Shakespeare Tercentenaries', combines late-Metaphysical ingenuity and love of conceit with an unmistakably late-Romantic demeanour, and thereby reveals something of the author's self-critical values, since she called it 'my one, my *one* masterpiece'.[7] 'Winter Trees on the Horizon' is so Victorian that it might seem perverse to compare its conceptual precision, its intellectual demands on the reader, its ability to make material specificities speak of larger, less palpable matters, with Donne or Marvell. But the comparison presents itself, and not only here but even in that poem's prose counterpart, the otherwise profoundly nineteenth-century essay on 'The Horizon'. And this elegant control of difficult imagery in coherent, sustained

---

7   Quoted in Badeni, p. 232.

conceit was already present in the passionate and personal early poems: 'Thoughts in Separation', which a casual reader hardly troubles to puzzle out, is a good example, while the brilliant pair of poems 'To the Beloved' and 'To the Beloved Dead', with their not-at-all-washy Romanticism, illustrate the point even better.

Another instance of her compact control of a single paradoxical idea, and one giving rather direct access to fundamental spiritual preoccupations, is the late poem 'To "A Certain Rich Man"', which finds a measure of redemption and human sympathy in the biblical parable of Dives and Lazarus, where most can find only cautionary menace and the bitter irony of comeuppance. Her paradox here is to emphasise the generosity, the 'ultimate human greatness', in the model villain. The elevation and traditional archaism of her diction is particularly apparent in this poem, which to some tastes may seem grandiose. But the poem has an epigrammatic focus and clarity, and the theme is a grand one after all. It touches powerfully on some of the aspects of her faith and morality that Meynell found most difficult. In a letter to her youngest son, who had approached her with doubts and troubles about the reality of eternal damnation, she had once written:

> Christ would not have told the story of 'the rich man' if there were nothing to fear. The atonement of our Saviour is not, however, fruitless, even for 'the rich man'. No doubt the wonderful unselfishness (in spite of a wholly selfish life on earth) that makes him in his place of exile and, no doubt, temporary pain, care for his brethren and wish them to be warned is something divine, won for him by Christ.[8]

---

8   Ms. Letter at Greatham, quoted in Badeni, p. 179.

In such a careful writer, even of familial letters, the second occurrence of the phrase 'no doubt' in a single sentence seems to waver between emphasis and misgiving. But Meynell sees 'eternal punishment', even for souls in heaven, in every person's regrets. 'I shall never cease to be sorry for some passages in my life, shall never cease to mourn for them', she says. 'All punishment is eternal, and all its consequences are eternal. We are subject to everlasting punishment because our deeds are irrevocable, because nothing can alter the past, and because we are ourselves for ever'. She is described by friends and family as self-critical, self-accusing, though she was neither self-effacing nor hampered by false modesty.

A poet devoted to clear, uncrowded focus of thought is bound to tend at times to the epigrammatic. In this anthology, 'Lord, I Owe Thee a Death' and '*Via, et Veritas, et Vita*' would fit the description of epigram, while other short pieces, such as 'I Am the Way', combine epigrammatic brevity, generality and conceptual singularity with the songlikeness and personal subjectivity usually associated with lyric. Of the latter description is one of her finest and most moving poems, 'Maternity'. This seems to me more or less perfect in its restraint and its trust in the bare import of what it has to say. Any further elaboration or sophistication would impair it, not only by encumbrance but by endangering the sharp simplicity of the pathos, which could otherwise become sentimental. The impersonality (not impartiality) of 'she' and 'they', and the detachment of quotation marks, guard it. The poem is not autobiographical, but Meynell had experienced the death of a child, her son Vivian, at the age of five months.

Still more obviously lyrical, but comparably brief and economical, is another rich poem connected with motherhood, the 'Cradle-Song at Twilight', one of Meynell's most imaginatively arresting poems. What a strange lullaby. This eight-line poem offers insight into three people: the child, the young nurse and the implied mother. It captures the child's reluctance to feel that twilight is night enough for sleeping, the girl's preoccupation with other thoughts and yearnings (the throbbing breast that sighs, in the evening, for 'other playfellows' than this baby she is asked to put to bed), and the way in which the girl's distraction is intuitively felt by the child as something not conducive to rest. And it evokes something of the child's playful attempt to retrieve that wandering attention; the similarity and divergence between the child's need for intimacy and the girl's grown-up or adolescent needs. Finally, implicitly, it registers a mother's sense of her own, different relation or attunement to her children, or perhaps to any children.

Having read the 'Cradle-Song' closely with many students, I can testify that what strikes most readers at first as a slight and straightforward, fluent lyric, nothing brambly about it, soon reveals the deceptiveness of its apparent simplicity and can fill hours of varied critical discussion. Is the nurse's 'unmaternal fondness' a fondness for the child, or is it the rival fondness for some other, grown-up playfellow? (The answer to the first question is surely Yes, but the second question does not seem irrelevant.) Is the poem built around a metaphor for twilight, the 'slender night', compared with 'too young a nurse'—as at first seems to be the case? But as the poem moves into its second half, it seems less a poem about night and more a poem about the young woman and the child. What is a metaphor for what? If the first metaphor is simply elaborating into a conceit, what are the other playfellows for which the *evening* sighs? (I suppose this registers the child's sense that everyone else is still awake and doing things.) And is the crepuscular time of nightfall less 'maternal' than the depths of night? Is Night a mother, a mother's embrace, a womb? The poem is full of suggestion, mysteriously evocative.

Occasionally even this very intellectual poet leaves overt reasoning aside altogether. 'The Rainy Summer' is an excellent example. It is not built around a paradox, thought and counterthought, a concept. It is a lyric of observational description, vivid in its imagery, wonderfully dynamic in rhythm and movement. But somehow one knows this is not mere impression-gathering for its own sake, not just description of the weather. For all the graphic and sensuous imagery, there is a sense of reticence; the three stanzas are saturated with human meanings held in check and made evocative. Perhaps this poem could be considered a sister to 'A Day and a Life' or 'A Comparison in a Seaside Field', the metaphors poignantly drawn out in those lyrics but left in quiet suggestion here. In any case the sensation of chill is powerfully conveyed, and it seems an interior chill as well as an external one. 'The rifled flowers are cold as ocean-shells': there is so much feeling soaked into this impersonal simile. 'The forest, rooted, tosses in her bonds'—another line of brilliant phonic delicacy; and another version, in another mood, of that tension of bonds and freedom envisaged in the bird metaphor of 'The Laws of Verse'.

Meynell often seems to leave things inexplicit, and she was always interested in silences. This is seen clearly in the two early poems 'To the Beloved'. The beloved is like the silence in every pause, 'A secret and a mystery / Between one footfall and the next'. Silence is the enveloping form of all sound; it is not the opposite of music, but music's very shape and surrounding element. The 'thought within all thought' is silence too. So her poems are made of music and thought, but also of silence.

Certain admirers, particularly those that knew her well, mention her reticence in person and the quality of silence in her writing. Patmore wrote to her, after a lively dinner party from which she was absent, 'I missed your silence',[9] while Meredith

9   Quoted in Viola Meynell, *Alice Meynell*, p. 146.

tells her in a letter: 'You write of your not being a talker. I can find the substance I want in your silences, and can converse with them'.[10] 'The footfalls of her Muse waken not sounds, but silences', Francis Thompson wrote, reviewing her poems: 'We lift a feather from the marsh and say "This way went a heron"'. According to Thompson, Meynell provided the age—and its mainly 'masculine poets'—with an important lesson, the 'law of silence'. What is the law? 'That high speech must be shod with silence, that high work must be set forth with silence, that high destiny must be waited on with silence'.[11] Meynell herself, meanwhile, in a touching essay on her memories of her father, who more than anyone else had helped to form her conscientiously intellectual habit of mind, calls him 'a man whose silence seems better worth interpreting than the speech of many another'.[12]

Her own style has sometimes been described as terse or laconic. The poems are generally thought to grow more so over the decades, whereas Viola Meynell makes the interesting observation that a different trajectory was taken by the prose—that her mother's earlier essays were marked by the kind of 'closeness and economy' one would expect in an author's later style. 'Youth, not age, was crabbed; age unlocked its words a little more liberally'.[13]

Minute and curious observation combined with the power of precise articulation made her able, in her prose work, to draw attention to subtle qualities of nature, art and experience, bringing clearly delineated new insight and perception to familiar things, and often then gently to

---

10   *Ibid.*, p. 129.

11   Francis Thompson, 'Mrs. Meynell's Poems', in *The Tablet* 81:2750 (21 Jan 1893), 89; quoted in Badeni, p. 97.

12   'A Remembrance', in *The Rhythm of Life* (1893), p. 12.

13   *Alice Meynell*, p. 75.

suggest larger implications or analogies. But characteristically this is done so that the concrete details are not narrowingly subordinated to the symbolism (which is rarely insistent), and nor is the symbolism an accidental or opportunistic addition to the concrete perceptions. Things are allowed to add up to greater meanings, moral or spiritual, according to the reader's readiness to follow. Unlike the Symbolist, at least in Arthur Symons's sense, she does not make the visible and external a hazy or phantasmagorical index to the invisible and internal, but is interested in it for its own sake, and sees it always as itself as well as an index to the larger things in which it partakes or to which it leads the mind. Look at the way she concludes the essay on 'Reflections'. Without dogmatism or blunt explicitness, this reflection on the literal reality of reflections rises to a spiritual contemplation and a divine metaphor which can be taken or left. I think that for her this was a natural progression, but none of the foregoing observation has been forcibly subsumed. Things are connected, sometimes surprisingly, but naturally, to other things. She is not a reductive writer but a connective one.

Compared with her friend Meredith she was never an exuberant prose stylist, but some of the later essays seem freer in their pursuit of a line of thinking, more content to dally in description and multiply illustration. This was partly a consequence of the different literary tasks to which she became habituated, since in 1893 she began to write a weekly unsigned column for the *Pall Mall Gazette* under the title 'The Wares of Autolycus', and this commitment, requiring a regular stream of fresh material, loosened her style into a more leisurely, though precise, species of belles-lettres. The 'Autolycus' articles were written by a small group of women writers who divided between themselves the days of the week, the *Pall Mall* being a daily publication. The other main authors were Violet Hunt, Graham R. Tomson (Rosamund

Marriott-Watson) and Elizabeth Robbins Pennell, the last of whom, an art critic who contributed humorous essays on gastronomy, refers to the 'Wares' as an 'entertaining array of unconsidered trifles', just as the title, alluding to *The Winter's Tale*, suggests.[14] All these columnists wrote well, and modesty should be taken for what it is, but that was the character of the column as Pennell saw it, and it is hard to imagine that Alice Meynell could quite have shared it—or that she could ever have sent in an essay she thought unconsidered or trivial. On the whole, as literature, her pieces were the most serious of the 'Wares'. Their standing out from the others was the circumstance that brought about her friendship with Meredith, who had written to her in admiration after having made enquiries as to the authorship of the Friday essays particularly.

Meynell's Autolycus essays on a range of topics continued for most of the rest of the 1890s. Essays such as 'Cloud', 'Shadows', 'Reflections', 'Nooks' and 'The Horizon'—roving but precise, and always with something of value to say—belong to that column. They are somewhat different in character from the compact expression of singular thoughts and arguments in earlier pieces such as 'The Rhythm of Life' (a justly praised and enviably articulated masterpiece of essayistic wisdom) or the more critically-minded essays on 'Pocket Vocabularies', 'Composure', 'The Point of Honour' and 'Rejection'. That last piece, as its theme both promises and ratifies, is a good exemplar and explanation of Meynell's conscious terseness, with its short, tense, sometimes gnomic sentences. Reticence and forthrightness can be partners; sometimes they may be hard to distinguish. Her more polemical essays have both qualities strongly in evidence, and her polemic is never that of

---

14   Elizabeth Robbins Pennell, *Nights: Rome, Venice, in the Aesthetic Eighties; London, Paris, in the Fighting Nineties* (1916), p. 158.

a simple type. Even in the Autolycus essays, however, Meynell could claim, in Meredith's opinion, 'the merit of saying just enough on the subject, leaving the reader to think'.[15]

As the essays became more open to wayward exploration and more welcoming to the significant associations that emerged around a central theme, the poems became more single-minded in focus—if this can be said of poems that so often adduce the alternative point of view. In most cases their austerity is not exactly an aspect of sparseness, but of control. Viola Meynell explains that her mother's literary aim, at least in later years, was for 'compact thought'.[16]

It is not a simple thing to show that Meynell is sparing with words. As her essays often multiply examples, angles and facets, many of her poems accumulate words and phrases, chains of items all belonging to the same grammatical category. 'And sign, approve, accept, conceive, create.' That is an extreme but very Meynellian line. Especially noticeable and characteristic are her sequences of adjectives or participles: 'Natural, true, keen', 'Unhoped, unsought!', 'Single, singular, apart',—

> Ignorant, innocent, instantaneous, free,
> Unwelcomed, unrenowned.

They are not always unbroken chains or long ones, and sometimes a strong pair—with some phonic quality in common or a semantic equivalence—suffices, especially where a paradox is to be pointed: 'Access, Approach'; 'The multiplied, / The ever unparted, whole'; 'Full of repose, full of replies'; 'Unnumbered man to the innumerable grave'. And of course

---

15 'Mrs. Meynell's Two Books of Essays' (*op. cit.*), p. 762; quoted also in a prefatory note to Meynell's *Wayfarings* (1929), p. 9.
16 *Alice Meynell*, p. 54.

these syntactical accumulations are often formed into more complex structures:

> The devout people, moved, intent, elate,
> And the devoted Lord.

This feature of her style, related to the bold verbal repetitions that she carried off so beautifully throughout her poetic work (consider the ends of 'Renouncement', 'After a Parting' and 'Easter Night'), has only vague antecedents in the early verse. But from the 1890s it becomes very distinct.

Some poems seem particularly to be constructed around these lists, groupings, balancings. 'In Portugal, 1912' moves almost ritually through its accumulated nouns—at first with their associated verbs (ll. 1-2), then alone (ll. 3-4), and later with their complementary adjectives (especially ll. 6-7)—before reaching an epigrammatic final quatrain. A yet starker illustration would be her poem 'In Manchester Square', which commemorates a London road-sweeper Meynell had befriended, passing by him each week in Marylebone. (Viola Meynell reproduces a touching letter her mother had written to this man once, explaining that she would not be passing through the square for a few weeks: 'I don't like to think you will forget me, nor do I like you to think I have forgotten you'.)[17] Each quatrain contains a strong stacking sequence or chain, twice with participles. The poem's stylistic character is strongly determined by this tendency—or principle.

Are these poems laconic, sparing of words, or is their terseness to be differently described? Reduction can be hard to tell from reinforcement. Ostensibly the words and the ideas they convey have been accumulated, multiplied; the thoughts gather, the words—especially when there are similarities

---

17   *Alice Meynell*, p. 241.

of sound—even seem to suggest and generate one another. Meynell's effect is neater and more classically restrained than that of Gerard Manley Hopkins—

> Earnest, earthless, equal, attuneable, | vaulty, voluminous, . . . stupendous[18]

—but it does share something of the same experimental reaching, sensuous as well as cerebral, through choice words for an imaginatively adequate meaning, and allowing the words that emerge from each other to remain alongside each other. On the other hand, against this sense of generative multiplication there is the sense, registered by most critics, of restraint, economy, compactness, the feeling that these listlike sequences are all that has been left of a complex thought that has been subject to a deliberate exclusion of surplusage. The choice words, stacked against each other, radiate associations and nuances upon which another poet might have spent additional lines and stanzas, but in Meynell they stand as a kind of evocative shorthand that trusts in the intelligence and imagination of readers. G.K. Chesterton said of her that she 'never wrote a line, or even a word, that does not stand like the rib of a strong intellectual structure; a thing with the bones of thought in it'.[19] Used to seeing more flesh on each bone, the reader may find her terse even when the ribs line up in ranks.

What are we seeing, then, a building-up or the end product of a boiling-down? Take these lines from 'The Launch'—

> Ah thus—not thus—the Dying, kissed,
> Cherished, exhorted, shriven, dismissed …

---

18   Hopkins, the opening of 'Spelt from Sibyl's Leaves'.

19   G.K. Chesterton, 'Alice Meynell', *Dublin Review* 172:344 (Jan-Mar 1923), 1-12; p. 3.

One can clearly make a strong case for the distinct and salient contribution of each item in the sequence; but in a short poem that also contains syntactical chains such as 'New weight, new force, new world', and 'we cling, we creep', the impression that we are dealing with a general feature of style and not in each case simply a capitulation to the needs of the thought is irresistible. It is a defining aspect of this poem, joining with its elevated, almost Johnsonian or Miltonic Latinity of diction: 'alien gravity', the grand roll of 'incalculable' in the final line. Do the poems grow more rhetorical? If so, is this because they are less exploratory, more certain of their aims, more intellectually determined? 'The Launch' illustrates the kind of work to which the terms 'rhetorical' and 'lyrical' seem equally suitable. On the lyrical side, it is a triumph of rhythm, cadence, bounce, dynamism, especially in its middle stanza; to some tastes it may even be too triumphant in this regard. On the rhetorical side, it relies heavily on very marked repeating structures and an undeniable grandiloquence. Overall it gives a very pronounced example of Alice Meynell's later verse style, although its obvious musicality distinguishes it from most of the poems of her final years. The poems, according to Viola Meynell, 'became deliberately less musical'.[20]

Even the most rhetorical of her poems, however, can claim all the complexity and unresolved tension of which lyric can be capable. 'The Two Questions' uses great oratorical drive to make one single point, but unlike most oratory it simplifies nothing: it raises something difficult to explain and hard to face. The final stanzas complete the thought with a masterful roundness, but they do not sound pat. They are brave in their squaring up to the 'cowardice' they own; they leave the moral problem stark and challenging. Is compassion cowardice? Knowing our own frailties, do we shudder at the punishments

---

20 *Alice Meynell*, p. 165.

of others only because we fear we deserve no better? Is it more virtuous to approve, as justice having nothing to do with us, the comeuppance of sinners, or to see ourselves as involved in the sins of the world and pity those who receive just deserts? Can we do both, and is either possible without egoism—whether of hypocrisy or self-pity? It would be possible to go on elaborating the questions so economically conjured by this poem. The intensity of its moral communication, in spite of rhetorical accumulation, is that of an authoritative reticence.

(ii) Alice Thompson: The Early Poems

The criterion of 'compact thought' brings us also to the question of the division between the 'earlier' and 'later' poems. In fact, 'earlier' here refers solely to those written up to the publication of *Preludes* in 1875, after which came two decades in which Meynell wrote very few poems and concentrated her energies on prose. Throughout most of her writing life she habitually insisted on this partitioning of her early verse, about which she had profound misgivings, from all the rest. In 1892, when those poems were reprinted with the small number of subsequent poems then written, she had been begged by Francis Thompson not to make extensive revisions. And when the collected volume of her poems was published in 1913, she wished for the early poems to be placed last in the book. Giving way on this matter, she formally introduced the 'Early' and 'Later' distinction, which was heralded in the Table of Contents and split the book into two sections. 'Oh, let the word *Early* be conspicuous!', she pleaded.[21]

---

21   Ms. letter (to Wilfrid Meynell) at Greatham, quoted in Badeni, p. 216; not in Atkinson's edition of *Selected Letters*.

It is almost as if the young Alice Thompson could dimly predict her own more mature view of those early poems, as if she feared the older woman's ironic belittlement of her youthful efforts and experiences. She attempted some insurance against this. One of the most memorable poems in *Preludes* is 'A Letter from a Girl to Her Own Old Age', a poignant mixture of earnest ingenuousness and considerable literary ingenuity, which enshrines some eloquent pleading for the remembrance of those adolescent experiences: that they were serious and real. 'Pardon the girl; such strange desires beset her'. (The uncertain tense of 'beset' is beautiful: do the desires seem strange already, or only from an imagined future retrospect?) To forestall the irony of the old woman looking back on distant youth, the girl adopts a kind of irony of her own in talking to her future self. I wonder if the Alice Meynell of later years felt a little embarrassed by this poem's demands on her indulgence, a little burdened by the emotional response she had already attributed to herself in the antepenultimate tercet ('O hush, O hush! Thy tears my words are steeping'). But I hope she felt also a motherly tenderness for the Thompson girl who had written the poem and spoke through it, not unmaternally, wondering how much of her 'wild heart' would survive the decades.

The early poems are much more Romantic in inspiration, showing the influence of Keats, Shelley and Tennyson, though with strong notes also of Elizabeth Barrett Browning. There are touches, here as later, of Elizabethan and seventeenth-century influence, not always very obviously via the Pre-Raphaelites, and sometimes quite persuasively *not* of that lineage. In large part they are passionate poems, often formed around a conflict between passion and will—the same tension that runs through so much of her work, but giving a more urgently personal impression here than later on, when the moral dramas would be presented in more general, paradigmatic ways. Although sometimes moving a step or two in the direction of 'dramatic lyric', as when an element of pastiche or fictive characterisation emerges, the early poems overall give us much more of the drama of the inner life and its privacy.

Like the 'Letter from a Girl to Her Own Old Age', the striking sonnet called 'The Young Neophyte' is spoken by a young woman looking forward with great seriousness over the rest of her life, identifying with her future self. The powerful sense of responsibility evoked there is characteristic. The poem is not autobiographical but, in a sense, an autobiographical fantasy. When Alice Thompson entered the Catholic Church she took responsibility for the rest of her life, for its conduct, its sacrifices and constraints—not those of a nun, but nevertheless a serious undertaking: the law containing the wildness. Here already is the poem of will, with the passion only glimpsed, suggested, latent. In other early poems, however, the passion is more fully, sensuously attested, the 'wild heart' more fully fleshed in the face of restraining willpower. And many of these were written under the stress of an intense and impossible love for the young Jesuit priest who had received her into the Roman Church in 1868.

Father Augustus Dignam was a highly cultured and literate man who encouraged Alice in her poetic gifts as well as in her faith. At the age of twenty she had known flirtations and longings before, as her diaries record; but this was a new experience, more lasting, and gave rise to some of her greatest poems. She loved him not only as a man but as a priest, a Catholic priest, celibate; to have achieved her desire for him in one aspect (had it even been within reach), would have been to lose a part of the object of that desire, and losing a part sometimes means losing the whole. To have gained Father Dignam as a husband or lover would have been to give up the 'Father', and in fact to have marred his spiritual vocation. From this impossible human situation she made poems of brilliant moral and emotional clarity, suffering with dignity in a composure that was self-denying in the sphere of action but never denying of the feelings left unsatisfied. When she speaks of 'the lack that lurks in all', it is with conviction, not only acquired Romantic wistfulness.

One of the most celebrated of the poems concerned with this crisis in her life is the sonnet 'Renouncement'—the one early poem that was not later renounced. It is interesting, then, that it was in fact omitted from *Preludes*, while other poems equally personal or revealing, such as 'Thoughts in Separation', were included. In 'Renouncement', the thought of the beloved 'lurks in all delight'. It must be avoided, however, not because it is bad and taints the delight, but because its unpossessable goodness, of a piece with 'blue Heaven' and with 'song' itself, is too much to bear without the possession that is not allowed. 'I must not think of thee'. 'I must stop short of thee the whole day long'. Yet between those two lines, which begin and end the octet with the same resolution, the figuration changes subtly: it is not she, the speaker, who must keep herself from moving close to this thought—the thought of the beloved—but rather the thought itself that threatens to come upon her. It 'lurks', as if with dubious intent; it 'waits hidden yet bright', as if glinting in the shadows; and 'it must never, never come in sight'. The thought, the internal beloved, with a life of its own that is not that of the real beloved, has its unpredictability, a vaguely sensed and uncertain motive. This expresses very well the ambiguous dynamics of the inner world, the tension of will and desire, and the situation in which even the good becomes almost menacing when it may neither be possessed nor forgotten.

The sestet that follows is a technical marvel of poetic movement, convincingly expressive of the struggle of conscious willpower to cope with the flooding power of what cannot always be kept at bay. Four lines, all single-moulded utterances that (significantly) do not run on but accumulate deliberately, deliberatively, their one central thought—amplifying, explaining, refiguring it—set up the tension: as if she were repeating and prolonging the thought, excusing her dreaming self as much as possible while postponing the dream for as long as possible. Sleep cannot be resisted, she 'must' loosen the bonds of the conscious mind, she 'must' take off her will as if she were taking off her daytime clothes (a courageous image).[22] In the final two lines, as sleep takes over and the unconscious begins its fuller reign, the tension releases. 'With the first dream that comes with the first sleep'—(is the drawn-out, repetitive phrasing of this beautiful line of monosyllables mere passionate emphasis, or the last, dissolving attempt to hold out?)—'I run, I run, I am gathered to thy heart'. Running as a river runs to the sea, or as a dye runs when it comes unfast, running passively, helplessly, in the medium of sleep or with its altered gravity. But also, of course, running as people run, actively, intentionally, to a goal. The repetition brings out both senses, the tension and confusion of agency. 'I run', 'I am gathered'.

Even in these early poems the images and conceits, or sometimes a single line or a closing thought, can be remarkably fresh and unanticipated. Sometimes the whole idea is a serious surprise gradually revealing itself, as in the brilliant sonnet 'To a Daisy'. Yet Meynell never seems to strain for novelty as a good in itself.

---

22   In 'Thoughts on War and Death' (1915), Sigmund Freud would arrive at almost exactly the same expressive simile: 'whenever we go to sleep we throw off our hard-won morality like a garment, and put it on again next morning. This stripping of ourselves is not, of course, dangerous, because we are paralysed, condemned to inactivity, by the state of sleep'. *SE XIV*, p. 286.

The 'Sonnet: To a Reader who should love me', with its strange syntax[23] and strange, hazy conceit—too hazy, I imagine, to pass muster with this very exacting author when she came to prepare her volume—is fascinating nonetheless, not only in its unusual route through imagery, but more generally in its rich and peculiar approach to what might look at first like a tamely conventional theme. As a reader who loves her, I have placed it first in the present selection. It imagines the future 'reader' as a beloved as well as one who loves. The young poet pines for the loving reader, though the face and embrace of that reader remain unrevealed to her: she has only her own substitutes for them, the grass and the earth of her garden, her poetry. The syntactical uncertainties the reader must navigate in the second quatrain of this sonnet can be resolved by thought as the conceit plays on, but perhaps indicate something of a fluidity of point of view, or of identification, almost as if she were occupying both positions at once, desired and desiring. One can see this also in her easy ambiguity with regard to poetic gender roles—in the wonderfully dynamic 'Wind-Song to the Hill', for instance, with or without the subtitle ('The Poet sings to a Maiden'); or in 'The Lover Urges the Better Thrift' or 'Your Own Fair Youth', both close to earlier models of male poets writing to women, while the latter also clearly recalls Shakespeare's homoerotic sonnets to the young man. In neither of these last cases did she feel the need, as with the 'Wind-Song', to elucidate the gender roles, even if later she would tell a correspondent that 'Your Own Fair Youth' was 'supposed to be addressed to a young

---

23 'A nightingale and loneliest of fire-flies / Palpitate in the darkness light and strain': in the same darkness a nightingale palpitates its (musical) strain while a fire-fly palpitates its light; or, probably, 'palpitate' follows 'shall sing' and is to be taken as '[shall] palpitate'. (In any case both the nightingale and the fire-fly are images of the 'young heart', in its twin aspects, respectively, as one that 'shall sing … and shine'.

woman by a lover'.[24] The result is an impression of confident liquidity in the positioning of the poetic persona with respect to literary traditions and traditional roles.

Meynell was a master especially of the stunning close. 'A Poet of One Mood', on a cursory first reading, contains some interesting images ('my harp of floods') but again perhaps looks overall like a relatively commonplace lyric of Romantic melancholy. The sestet appears only to amplify or repeat the sense of the octet, until the strange, totally compelling images of the last two lines:

> A small cloud full of rain upon my heart
> And in mine arms, clasped, like a child in tears.

This composite image conveys so immediately the volatility of held emotion on the brink of release. The first part, the little cloud—not *in* the heart but *upon* it, already externalized—is itself a sufficiently powerful metaphor to express saturation of feeling, fulness that could deliquesce at any moment; but the continuation, in which the cloud is held like a loved person in an embrace, a child, and the rain is finally let out in tears, mysteriously catches at the complexity of real emotion. The cloud is a substitute for the absent love, but it is also a child in tears, and the tears are the poet's own, displaced into cloud and child; so that the child is a part or version of herself, the part that does not need to hold the cloud safe, as stable vapour, but can weep and be comforted. The embrace at the same time suggests the imagined and impossible embrace of the beloved and the self-embrace of a person consoling themselves. Lover and beloved again become confused, and the responsibility towards the crying child is ambiguous. Tears or no tears, the clasping holds it all together.

---

24   From a letter to an unknown recipient, dated August 14 [no year], in private ownership.

In 'The Visiting Sea', with its more sustained and complex conceit, again Meynell proves her command of daring, unexpected endings that bring large emotional force. The last line is a risk that raises the whole poem with its strange poignancy, the apparently simple phrasing and its difficult, mysterious thought. And I remember reading 'Thoughts in Separation' for the first time, hardly thinking it worth the expenditure of intellectual attention that its talk of 'guardian spirits' actually requires, and lazily suspecting the whole thing of polite conventionality, pious sentiment, vagueness, until the last line came like thunder. I would call it a shocking line: the stark image of the material cross and the beloved's kissing it in worship; the poignantly counterbalanced image of the poet, a young woman, kissing her mother, where the poignancy contains the possibility of a bitter pathos amid its rueful tenderness. The kiss of the penultimate line, given the abstract, angelic imaginings that have led up to it, seems at first an ethereal, hypothetical thing, and in that last line suddenly becomes physical—but two kisses, not one. And yet it is willed, through the flight of speculative fancy, into becoming a divided substitute for the shared physical kiss that must be forgone. Was she thinking of Crashaw's lines of mystical eroticism in the 'Hymn to St Teresa', who, as a girl, burns with love for Christ?—

> Her weak breast heaves with strong desire
> Of what she may with fruitless wishes
> Seek for amongst her mother's kisses.

The sense of erotic longing and spiritual striving, in Meynell's case not one and the same thing but painfully conflicting, is bravely expressed. There is something shatteringly stark about the cadence of her closing line—a pentameter of four hard stresses—and its sharp division in two.

She had her gift for poetic surprise, then, from an early age, and her surprises are no tricks but intensely meaningful. In 'The Garden', one more early sonnet that at first seems typical ('My heart shall be thy garden'), there is a sober moral value to the final movement of thought, more penetratingly truthful than a mediocre poet would offer. And this makes all the difference. As birds fly from a garden, so—

> My heart has thoughts, which, though thine eyes
>   hold mine,
> Flit to the silent world and other summers,
> With wings that dip beyond the silent seas.

This honest reservation cuts through what a simpler sentimentality would think sufficient, and tells the truth about the limits of what can be given. It makes a reservation of her liberty of thought—thoughts of the heart—which cannot be held or pledged. The evocative final images celebrate freedom and privacy. This is expressive of Meynell's sense of human dignity, the importance of solitude, silence and untrammelled selfhood, even when so much of the self is given lovingly to others. It is characteristic also of her refusal of the easy sentiment that can be proven insincere. So also in 'The Visiting Sea', with a mixture of teasing pride and the confidence that she will be understood and respected, she writes to the beloved: 'What! I have secrets from you? Yes'.

(iii) Character and Convictions

With her generosity and her formidable conscientiousness in moral and aesthetic matters (which cannot have been neatly separated in her mind), Alice Meynell became a valuable resource to many of her literary friends, and of course to her readers. She was a writer of strong convictions but also sympathetic tolerance—not so much of human frailties, strictly speaking, as of frail human beings. She worked hard, not in leisure but for a living, and all the harder because much of her work was done to a standard far higher than that purpose on its own would have demanded: she was immensely self-critical, but justly confident and proud of at least some of her achievements. Her pride was certainly not spiritual pride. Like many people known for high-mindedness and rectitude, however, she could sometimes be found austere, aloof, inaccessible.

As a writer and critic she could indeed be loftily ironic, using sarcasm and scorn in the service not only of good morality, as she saw it, but also good taste and sound thinking. This was a part of her literary personality, particularly in prose. It is strong in 'Rejection' and 'Pocket Vocabularies', shows more touchingly in defence of the dignity of 'Prue' and 'Mrs. Johnson', and emerges here and there with an accompanying note of self-directed comicality somewhat undercutting the high-handedness. (An example would be the end of the essay on 'Nooks'.) Still, throughout her work and the records of her personal life, a commitment to fairness and a scrupulousness to avoid hypocrisy are very clear, and in the essays just mentioned on the derision popularly levelled at the wives of Richard Steele and Dr. Johnson—the one for being a supposed nag and scold, the other for being twenty-one years her husband's senior—it was in the service of fairness and respect, and against facile and scoffing judgementalism, that her irony was so movingly enlisted.

She could be roguish, tease and be teased, though her sense of humour was modulated by her strict unwillingness to take unkind or dishonourable advantage. She combined moral uprightness and spiritual seriousness with a humane involvement in worldly experience, its fun and its less harmful vanities. Though never quite in step with the latest styles, she did not disdain fashion or affect unfashionability but was elegant and took pride in her appearance. In many ways anxious to respect the social proprieties, her eccentrically bohemian upbringing, beginning in Italy, made middle-class British ways and the decorum of London society a little less than second nature to her. She disliked any extravagance in food, for moral reasons, but loved diamond jewellery. This combination of qualities was evidently both charming and inspiring, personally as well as in what she wrote. And for all the apparent austerity and reserve, she could acknowledge a taste for risk, confessing to a strange pleasure and excitement in danger—even during air raids or when carried over a bank by bolting cab-horses—and she speaks repeatedly of her delight in motorcars and fast driving.

Again and again she mentions her 'wild heart', which is allowed its wildness within strict bounds. Living in avowed submission to a moral code taken from Catholic dogma and followed 'to the letter', she was serious-minded, though not solemn, and kept a check on her passions. Friends and family record that she was very reserved about her deeper feelings, worries and regrets. Letters and diaries, after the more passionate forthcomingness of her youth, give a similar impression. But as far as one can tell from her literary work, she seems to have remained remarkably well in touch with the aspects of her experience that her self-control kept from becoming real risks. Instead of denying inner experience, she made conscious refusals in the outer realm of action. In her writing, which constituted a middle ground, the conflict is productive and moving.

Surveying her biography, one is struck by the degree to which confidence in the control of conduct allowed for feelings, not hers alone, to be openly acknowledged and expressed. She had intimate, romantic friendships, most intensely with Coventry Patmore, but also notably with George Meredith in his final years. The great Catholic poet

Francis Thompson, whom the Meynells virtually took in from the streets, publishing his work and caring for his welfare for the rest of his life, was ardent in his love for her, both erotic and filial, entirely without hope or demand for reciprocation. And this was freely manifest in daily communications as well as in his verse: manifest to others in the family circle, not only to his beloved Mrs. Meynell. Circumstances such as these would have frightened or scandalized many another in her position, or indeed her husband's; but in fact there seems to have been no suspicion, no nervous denial, and in Wilfrid Meynell no resentment or jealousy, until Patmore's pitch of feeling became too great and that intimacy had to be broken off—and even then we have no right, given what scant evidence there is, to infer those bitter sentiments on Wilfrid's part. It seems that they all, notwithstanding Patmore's uncertain expectations, had such confidence in Alice's integrity, and also, for much of the time, in one another's, that emotions and their expression in words were given great latitude in accordance with the certainty of ultimate restraint. This would seem to be only one aspect of Alice Meynell's whole approach to life, which is evident in her writing too.

'Safeguard' was a favourite word of hers, as letters in particular show. Religion and its dogma provided a moral safeguard, and there was a morality of the aesthetic and the intellectual too, needing other safeguards. The essay on 'Composure' speaks of ethical needs in literary style. 'The Point of Honour' gives the measure of her sense of the responsibilities of art and of criticism. In prose as well as verse she was a poet of responsibility, principle, conviction, balance, second thoughts. Her manner, and sometimes, especially in the early work, her theme, could be described by the phrases 'restrained passion' or 'passionate restraint'. But the obverse of her responsibility was an acknowledged yearning for acceptable forms of irresponsibility. The poem 'To Sleep' lets out the inexorable wish, deep down, for 'Liberty, liberty, from this weight of will', and ends with the plea: 'Make me all night the innocent fool that dreams'. In 'Renouncement' it is in the irresponsibility of dream-life that the will is put aside, without blame, and the lover can run to her beloved's arms.

Included among her responsibilities, in addition to those of art and criticism, were her political responsibilities as a woman, a Christian and Catholic woman, and a woman writer. She had felt at an early age the injustice of inequalities between the sexes, as her adolescent diaries show:

> Answer O World, man-governed, man-directed, answer for the sanity of your laws and your morals. Of all the crying evils in this depraved earth, ay, of all the sins of which the cry must surely come to Heaven, the greatest, judged by all the laws of God and of Humanity, is the miserable selfishness of men that keeps women from work.[25]

Women should have work for the mind to save them from 'a miserably self-conscious melancholy which feeds upon itself'—or worse fates. 'This is my demand for myself and for my sisters', she wrote, adding a sentiment that would not survive her youth: 'O my Shelley, if you were alive you would help me to fulfil my golden dream and the earth might taste happiness for once'. Later, with the confidence of mature artistry (and, by the way, rather more mixed feelings about Shelley), she was an eloquent and active advocate for the rights and dignity of woman. Her public letters and newspaper articles on political topics are intellectually as well

---

25   From a ms. diary at Greatham; quoted in Badeni, p. 28, and more selectively in Viola Meynell, *Alice Meynell*, pp. 37-38.

as rhetorically cogent, balanced, fair, nuanced, respectful of the varieties of opinion within certain limits but refusing to regard all matters as merely matters of opinion. One such letter on 'Catholics and Women's Suffrage', published in *The Tablet* in 1912, is a fine example of her ability to combine stinging sarcasm with brilliant precision and clarity of reasoning.

> Your correspondent L.S. takes upon himself the task of hooting Christian women from the path of their duty, as they have the right to understand it. 'No Christian woman', he writes, 'can be a Suffragette and remain a Christian'. The reason he gives for this grotesque dogma is that wives are bound to obey their husbands 'in all things consistent with Christian piety'. The connexion of ideas is remote. (It may be said incidentally that many women in Christendom do not marry. How much obedience to other women's husbands does L.S. hold St. Peter and St. Paul to impose upon these? To whose husband did Miss Jex Blake, one of the earliest and chief leaders of our movement, who died unmarried, owe obedience? Whose should St. Catherine of Siena have obeyed? Whose, Joan of Arc? The imagination reels.) […] Yet, assuming this connexion between conjugal obedience and the franchise of women, it is a tenable opinion that a woman cannot consistently with Christian piety abstain from demanding a share in the making and execution of laws at a time when legislation and public opinion virtually condone infamous crimes against women and young children. Condone them, I say, by the infliction of trifling fines and light and brief imprisonments. And this is done daily in the police courts. To demand

a share in legislation, and in the public formation of public opinion is so clearly the duty of Christian women that I might be tempted to retort upon L.S.'s insufferable doctrine with 'No woman can refuse to be a Suffragette and remain a Christian'. But (unlike your correspondent) I have a respect for the consciences that are unlike my own. I may add that the Archbishop of San Francisco has issued a pastoral to women voters the sense of which is nearer to that of the sentence I do not pronounce than to that of the sentence which L.S. pronounces so insolently.[26]

I give this extract as an instance of her more topical journalism. 'Victorian Caricature', 'The Woman in Grey', 'Prue' and 'Mrs. Johnson', meanwhile, are examples in the present selection of Meynell's more essayistic handling of matters related to 'feminism'—she uses the new-coined word herself, with cautious quotation marks, though not disowning its meaning.

With her Victorian sense of decorum, her Catholic moral seriousness and the touch of saintliness with which others often imbued her, Alice Meynell was not always wholeheartedly taken up by the women writers and intellectuals of subsequent generations, and her devotion to the poetry of Coventry Patmore, the author of *The Angel in the House* with its very 'Victorian' ideal of wifely domesticity (although Meynell found the later and less famous *Odes* much greater), has sometimes counted against her. Some remarks about her in Virginia Woolf's diary are so full of venomous projection that reprinting them seems a disservice to both writers. And yet even Vita Sackville-West, who in different ways loved them both, sees Meynell's opinions on women—and on women's

---

26   *The Tablet* 120:3782 (2 Nov 1912), 704; reprinted in *Selected Letters*, ed. Atkinson, pp. 323-34.

contribution to the arts—as 'very much in line with the views later expressed by Virginia Woolf in *A Room of One's Own*'.[27] As for Patmore, Meynell wrote to him in a letter, reproduced in Viola Meynell's *Memoir*:

> It has been a happiness to read again, through and through, the words of the greatest intellect I have ever known. To me the truth of your teaching is much more than convincing, it is evident instantly; the only effort I have to make is to understand—a most happy effort. But why is it that some passages—a very few and all in the later book—trouble me by getting no interior assent from me at all? . . .

The ellipsis is in the text as given by Viola Meynell, and the letter then continues along a different line.[28] Actually the ellipsis is an example of tact in Viola. Returning to the original letter, one finds that only a single sentence was thus omitted. It reads: 'They are all about women'.[29]

There were other important responsibilities too, among them the more personal ones of family and friendship, and these also are felt in her writings. In particular she became known as an insightful writer on children and motherhood (which may have something to do with the tendency in some later writers to identify this busy and independent-spirited professional writer with the housewifely ideal of the 'angel in the house'). 'Near the Ground' and the pair of essays on 'The Child of Tumult', inspired by her youngest son, Francis, represent such topics in this selection, though there were many

---

27 *Centenary Volume*, p. 22.

28 *Alice Meynell*, p. 114.

29 Quoted in Badeni, p. 95; not in Atkinson.

other essays and two whole volumes published in her lifetime, not to mention the various poems that touch on similar themes. 'It is something of an achievement to write on dangerously sentimental subjects', says Sackville-West again, 'without provoking even one anticipated quiver of embarrassment in the reader'.[30] 'Parentage' might be accused of 'sentiment', but of a kind set up, in the terrible apprehension of a certain mood, against the more common sentimentalities. Put beside it 'The Modern Mother', in which the mother—'giver of life, peace, death, distress'—desires from her child 'not so much / Thanks as forgiveness'. And set that, in turn, next to '*Veni Creator*', her greatest and bravest religious poem, in which God himself, like the mother, has something to be forgiven by his creatures. Meynell has looked hard at these hard things from different points of view and there is nothing easy about them.

But it is not simply a question of readerly 'embarrassment'. 'In all ages', the psychoanalyst and paediatrician D.W. Winnicott has written, 'there are the few who believe in the little child's feelings, and the majority who deny or sentimentalize'.[31] Alice Meynell may be proposed as a member of the few. In an important way, the poem 'Intimations of Mortality' positions itself against the defensive illusions of ignorance and innocence that parents find comfortable, and in which children are expected to become complicit. The wider corollaries and analogies are expansive. Meynell admired Barrie's *Peter Pan* but deplored the custom in stage performances of making the children chant 'I *do* believe in fairies', in order to revive Tinkerbell: this, she said, was a sentimental imposition onto children of an adult fantasy of what childhood is like, 'a game of men and women at the expense of children'.

---

30 *Centenary Volume*, p.18.

31 'Mental Hygiene in the Pre-School Child', unpublished, 1930s, quoted in Adam Phillips, *Winnicott* (1988, 2007), p. 48.

We are indeed child's-playing with serious things
and with serious words when we ask our children to
say they believe in fairies. Not that our request will
ever make them believe; they are honest people. But
in this appeal we tamper with the word 'believe,' and
palter with its sense.[32]

She is wary of the 'sentimental humour' that fastens on
children, and although her prose writings on childhood are
full of humour and tenderness, they recognise the dignity of
the child and the seriousness of the child's experience. 'Only
to a trivial eye is there nothing tragic in the sight of these
great passions within the small frame, the small will, and, in
a word, the small nature', she writes in 'The Child of Tumult'.
'He knows thus much—that life is troubled around him and
that the fates are strong'. The note of irony there is delicately
balanced; it does not ridicule.

One other title, included here, deserves mention among
her writings on children, partly because it is addressed,
unusually, *to* a child, and partly also because it gives a glimpse
of Meynell's feelings about the black ancestry she had on
the paternal side. This is the poem 'To O——, of Her Dark
Eyes', written for her daughter Olivia. Alice's father, Thomas
Thompson, was the illegitimate son of a James Thompson,
himself in turn the illegitimate son of a Thomas Pepper
Thompson who had emigrated to Jamaica and owned
sugar plantations there. The younger Thomas was brought
to England as a child, is traditionally thought to have been
educated at Cambridge (although records are lacking), and
later was able to support his family on the inheritance from
his grandfather. His mother (and Alice's grandmother), Mary
Edwards, is described as 'Creole' and was of mixed race.

---

32   *Childhood* (1913), pp. 31-32.

The poem to Olivia reads the child's dark eyes—'this lovely darkness', unusual in the family—as a generation-skipping inheritance from unknown ancestors far in the past and across 'tropic seas'. It is a poem about what is 'forgotten' and not forgotten, and somewhere in that tension may lie a difficult remembrance of the social conditions under which, in the plantations of the West Indies in the age of slavery, mixed-race children usually came into the world. But there is a sense of pride in this distant non-European ancestry, and if the poem can be accused of sentimentalism, it may at least be remembered that this was far from the common sentiment of Meynell's time and milieu.

*

It would be wrong to separate all of Alice Meynell's moral responsibilities—to God and her religion, to fellow women, to her family and friends, to justice—from those that governed her artistic work. Her aesthetic and intellectual responsibilities were felt as moral ones also, founded in convictions. Her fastidiousness and intellectualism were not of the academic kind, and she did not delight in shows of arcane knowledge or pyrotechnic wit. But she is a writer who makes significant demands on the reader, even if they are quiet demands, easy for a cursory, impressionistic reading to miss. I have seen many readers breeze through 'Winter Trees on the Horizon' or 'A Day and a Life', thinking they were reading something much hazier and more stereotyped than was really the case, and then gradually having to realize how much they had missed. The latter poem's spry lyricism (it is a rare departure from iambics) can sweep one along so that the precision of the conceit and its various elements are skipped over; but in fact the poem asks for a vivid apprehension of the angles of sun and shadow on different surfaces at different times of day, even before one comes to the metaphorical interpretation. It is a triumph. The former poem, meanwhile, casually requires its reader to think quite clearly about the effect of the curvature of the earth, in conjunction with the altitude of the point of view, on the distance of the horizon, and to conceptualise this imaginatively and symbolically.

Perhaps 'demand' is the wrong word, and it is more a case of expectant provision. In the poems, especially, modern readers often find more than they anticipate, but only if they read carefully enough to recognise the appeals made to their own clear thinking. 'Necessarily, where an intellect is at work, ours should be active', Meredith counsels in an appreciation of her work.[33] But the thinking is not chilly. It is sensuous and emotionally subtle. Francis Thompson conceived it strikingly when he spoke of her poems' characteristic of 'imaginative thought with feeling murmuring about its base'.[34]

The young Alice Thompson, before she had published any of her poems, wrote to the Irish poet William Allingham, inviting him to be unsparing in his critique of her work. She did not want 'praise' but 'hard words' about her faults. As examples she lists a number of artistic sins, including 'sickliness, want of tone, indefiniteness of expression'. But a parenthesis inserted just here strikes a note, even as early as that, of pride and confidence in one area: '(indefiniteness of thought I won't admit)'.[35] She was already writing things as conceptually sharp and fresh as 'To a Daisy', 'To the Beloved' and 'To the Beloved Dead', and knew she had control of what D.G. Rossetti would call the 'fundamental brainwork' of the poet.

---

33 'Mrs. Meynell's Two Books of Essays' (*op. cit.*), p. 763.

34 'Mrs. Meynell's Poems', (*op. cit.*), p. 89.

35 Quoted in Badeni, p. 50; not in Atkinson.

Her writings are comforting in their generous and careful humanity, but confronting in their unsentimental analysis of human life and their squaring up to hard questions. They are winning in their stylishness, confidence and humour; difficult, through their refusal to condescend to the reader with explanations that could be spared; impressive and enriching with the clarity and subtlety of her observations, often minute, sometimes technical, but almost always turned towards a larger idea or insight. She mixes challenge with charm, and can enjoy—especially in her essays—scintillation, as if for its own sake, without ever being content to leave it at that. And she can be deeply poignant, in a peculiar way that a more sentimental or a less intellectually exigent author could not have achieved.

PART I

POEMS

SONNET

To a Reader who should love me

Come in the year's mid-summer and in thine,
Into the deep soft midnight for a space,
'Mong wild closed flowers and wheat, a meek tilled place
Of folded poppies, maize, and rills of vine.
There, young and mournful, in this realm of mine,
With only a little growing grass for thy face,
Only the labouring earth for thine embrace
All my young heart shall sing for thee and shine;
A nightingale and loneliest of fire-flies
Palpitate in the darkness light and strain,
Tho' thine own stars be stifled in soft skies,
And thine own music mute, for any pain.
And I have dews to wet thy quiet eyes
Till thou forsake me for thy life again.

June 1869

WIND-SONG TO THE HILL

(The Poet Sings to a Maiden)

How shall I climb thee, hill of flowers and clover?
—I muse with cloud-wings furled against the sun.
A pause too still for earth hath stolen over.
In the divine quiet, Nature, little one,
Draws breath before the coming of thy lover.

Say, shall I come with wings from plains of flowers
Where poets' thoughts make a rain-bow wilderness?
Shall I bring songs from where the diamond showers
And grey skies mix the sun with tenderness?
And shall the souls of many larks be ours?

Or shall I tell thee of the midmost wailing
Of an indignant and unpitied sea?
Wet thee with what did wet me of the unfailing
Long wave-despairs that fare forsakenly,
Passion with pain that follows unavailing?

Over the round hill-tops shall I come to thee,
High-hearted, with light feet upon the thyme,
A child, an impulse sprung from spring to woo thee,
Young with all youth, O hill that I would climb,
With morning thoughts from Morning throned to sue thee?

Shall I rend clouds for garments to enfold thee,
Bind round thy brows the bent and crying skies?
Darkened with my dark hours shall I behold thee
Through all the great rains of my passionate eyes?
With arms of pain and tempest shall I hold thee?

Shall I come cold with news of dawn, o'ertaking
The tired stars? From my soul's sleep shall I call
Things that we guess not?—as the bird half-waking
Sings out of dreams those deepest songs of all
From some unknown sleep-heaven i' the dark day-breaking?

Shall I be all but silence, fitfully failing
Flickering in pale air like a dying light?
Shall I come as the west wind cometh, trailing
The day's gold robes thro' half the heavenly night,
Till round thy brows all the cold east is paling?

Or shall I be the fervid South-wind for thee?
Summer-long thro' the sunlights shall I stream?
Swift, but serene as beauty blow before thee,
Move among all the still stars with my dream,
Bring souls of deep South-summers to adore thee?

Shall I storm, love-strong, thy small wildernesses,
Thy humble heights, bare to all suns and showers?
Sport with thy timorous thoughts and poet-guesses,
Shaking thy shortest grass and little flowers,
Rioting in thy dreamiest lonelinesses?

—Or loiter where thy longest lawn reposes,
Where the dim plain is gentlest from thy feet,
Wait thy slow sweetness, watch as it uncloses,
Tarry thy silence, quiet with pale June heat,
Wait for the opening of thy wan wild roses?

—Oh, with a pæan of sound I will renown thee,
With waves of lights and shadows I will drown thee.
And like a wind, a wild wind I will crown thee.

March 1869

THE GARDEN

My heart shall be thy garden. Come, my own,
   Into thy garden; thine be happy hours
   Among my fairest thoughts, my tallest flowers,
From root to crowning petal thine alone.
Thine is the place from where the seeds are sown
   Up to the sky enclosed, with all its showers.
   But ah, the birds, the birds! Who shall build bowers
To keep these thine? O friend, the birds have flown.

For as these come and go, and quit our pine
   To follow the sweet season, or, new-comers,
   Sing one song only from our alder-trees,
My heart has thoughts, which, though thine eyes hold mine,
   Flit to the silent world and other summers,
   With wings that dip beyond the silver seas.

A LETTER FROM A GIRL TO HER OWN OLD AGE

Listen, and when thy hand this paper presses,
O time-worn woman, think of her who blesses
What thy thin fingers touch, with her caresses.

O mother, for the weight of years that break thee!
O daughter, for slow time must yet awake thee,
And from the changes of my heart must make thee!

O fainting traveller, morn is grey in heaven.
Dost thou remember how the clouds were driven?
And are they calm about the fall of even?

Pause near the ending of thy long migration,
For this one sudden hour of desolation
Appeals to one hour of thy meditation.

Suffer, O silent one, that I remind thee
Of the great hills that stormed the sky behind thee,
Of the wild winds of power that have resigned thee.

Know that the mournful plain where thou must wander
Is but a grey and silent world, but ponder
The misty mountains of the morning yonder.

Listen:—the mountain winds with rain were fretting,
And sudden gleams the mountain-tops besetting.
I cannot let thee fade to death, forgetting.

What part of this wild heart of mine I know not
Will follow with thee where the great winds blow not,
And where the young flowers of the mountain grow not.

Yet let my letter with thy lost thoughts in it
Tell what the way was when thou didst begin it,
And win with thee the goal when thou shalt win it.

Oh, in some hour of thine thy thoughts shall guide thee.
Suddenly, though time, darkness, silence, hide thee,
This wind from thy lost country flits beside thee,—

Telling thee: all thy memories moved the maiden,
With thy regrets was morning over-shaden,
With sorrow, thou hast left, her life was laden.

But whither shall my thoughts turn to pursue thee?
Life changes, and the years and days renew thee.
Oh, Nature brings my straying heart unto thee.

Her winds will join us, with their constant kisses
Upon the evening as the morning tresses,
Her summers breathe the same unchanging blisses.

And we, so altered in our shifting phases,
Track one another 'mid the many mazes
By the eternal child-breath of the daisies.

I have not writ this letter of divining
To make a glory of thy silent pining,
A triumph of thy mute and strange declining.

Only one youth, and the bright life was shrouded.
Only one morning, and the day was clouded.
And one old age with all regrets is crowded.

O hush, O hush! Thy tears my words are steeping.
O hush, hush, hush! So full, the fount of weeping?
Poor eyes, so quickly moved, so near to sleeping?

Pardon the girl; such strange desires beset her.
Poor woman, lay aside the mournful letter
That breaks thy heart; the one who wrote, forget her:

The one who now thy faded features guesses,
With filial fingers thy grey hair caresses,
With morning tears thy mournful twilight blesses.

THE YOUNG NEOPHYTE

Who knows what days I answer for to-day?
   Giving the bud I give the flower. I bow
   This yet unfaded and a faded brow;
Bending these knees and feeble knees, I pray.
Thoughts yet unripe in me I bend one way,
   Give one repose to pain I know not now,
   One check to joy that comes, I guess not how.
I dedicate my fields when Spring is grey.

O rash! (I smile) to pledge my hidden wheat.
   I fold to-day at altars far apart
Hands trembling with what toils? In their retreat
   I seal my love to-be, my folded art.
I light the tapers at my head and feet,
   And lay the crucifix on this silent heart.

THOUGHTS IN SEPARATION

We never meet; yet we meet day by day
   Upon those hills of life, dim and immense—
   The good we love, and sleep, our innocence.
O hills of life, high hills! And, higher than they,
Our guardian spirits meet at prayer and play.
   Beyond pain, joy, and hope, and long suspense,
   Above the summits of our souls, far hence,
An angel meets an angel on the way.

Beyond all good I ever believed of thee
   Or thou of me, these always love and live.
And though I fail of thy ideal of me,
My angel falls not short. They greet each other.
   Who knows, they may exchange the kiss we give,
Thou to thy crucifix, I to my mother.

A POET OF ONE MOOD

A poet of one mood in all my lays,
    Ranging all life to sing one only love,
    Like a west wind across the world I move,
Sweeping my harp of floods mine own wild ways.
The countries change, but not the west-wind days
    Which are my songs. My soft skies shine above,
    And on all seas the colours of a dove,
And on all fields a flash of silver greys.

I make the whole world answer to my art
    And sweet monotonous meanings. In your ears
I change not ever, bearing, for my part,
    One thought that is the treasure of my years—
A small cloud full of rain upon my heart
    And in mine arms, clasped, like a child in tears.

TO THE BELOVED

Oh, not more subtly silence strays
    Amongst the winds, between the voices,
Mingling alike with pensive lays,
    And with the music that rejoices,
Than thou art present in my days.

My silence, life returns to thee
    In all the pauses of her breath.
Hush back to rest the melody
    That out of thee awakeneth;
And thou, wake ever, wake for me!

Thou art like silence all unvexed,
    Though wild words part my soul from thee.
Thou art like silence unperplexed,
    A secret and a mystery
Between one footfall and the next.

Most dear pause in a mellow lay!
    Thou art inwoven with every air.
With thee the wildest tempests play,
    And snatches of thee everywhere
Make little heavens throughout a day.

Darkness and solitude shine, for me.
    For life's fair outward part are rife
The silver noises; let them be.
    It is the very soul of life
Listens for thee, listens for thee.

O pause between the sobs of cares;
    O thought within all thought that is;
Trance between laughters unawares:
    Thou art the shape of melodies,
And thou the ecstasy of prayers!

TO THE BELOVED DEAD

A Lament

Beloved, thou art like a tune that idle fingers
      Play on a window-pane.
The time is there, the form of music lingers;
      But O thou sweetest strain,
Where is thy soul? Thou liest in the wind and rain.

Even as to him who plays that idle air,
      It seems a melody,
For his own soul is full of it, so, my Fair,
      Dead, thou dost live in me,
And all this lonely soul is full of thee.

Thou song of songs!—not music as before
      Unto the outward ear;
My spirit sings thee inly evermore,
      Thy falls with tear on tear.
I fail for thee, thou art too sweet, too dear.

Thou silent song, thou ever voiceless rhyme,
      Is there no pulse to move thee,
At windy dawn, with a wild heart beating time,
      And falling tears above thee,
O music stifled from the ears that love thee?

Oh, for a strain of thee from outer air!
      Soul wearies soul, I find.
Of thee, thee, thee, I am mournfully aware,
      —Contained in one poor mind,
Who wert in tune and time to every wind.

Poor grave, poor lost belovèd! but I burn
     For some more vast To be.
As he that played that secret tune may turn
     And strike it on a lyre triumphantly,
I wait some future, all a lyre for thee.

THE VISITING SEA

As the inhastening tide doth roll,
Home from the deep, along the whole
   Wide shining strand, and floods the caves,
   —Your love comes filling with happy waves
The open sea-shore of my soul.

But inland from the seaward spaces,
None knows, not even you, the places
   Brimmed, at your coming, out of sight,
   —The little solitudes of delight
This tide constrains in dim embraces.

You see the happy shore, wave-rimmed,
But know not of the quiet dimmed
   Rivers your coming floods and fills,
   The little pools 'mid happier hills,
My silent rivulets, over-brimmed.

What! I have secrets from you? Yes.
But, visiting Sea, your love doth press
   And reach in further than you know,
   And fills all these; and, when you go,
There's loneliness in loneliness.

YOUR OWN FAIR YOUTH

Your own fair youth, you care so little for it—
    Smiling towards Heaven, you would not stay the advances
    Of time and change upon your happiest fancies.
I keep your golden hour, and will restore it.
If ever, in time to come, you would explore it—
    Your old self, whose thoughts went like last year's pansies,
    Look unto me; no mirror keeps its glances;
In my unfailing praises now I store it.

To guard all joys of yours from Time's estranging,
    I shall be then a treasury where your gay,
      Happy, and pensive past unaltered is.
I shall be then a garden charmed from changing,
    In which your June has never passed away.
      Walk there awhile among my memories.

IN EARLY SPRING

O Spring, I know thee! Seek for sweet surprise
    In the young children's eyes.
But I have learnt the years, and know the yet
    Leaf-folded violet.
Mine ear, awake to silence, can foretell
    The cuckoo's fitful bell.
I wander in a grey time that encloses
    June and the wild hedge-roses.
A year's procession of the flowers doth pass
    My feet, along the grass.
And all you wild birds silent yet, I know
    The notes that stir you so,
Your songs yet half devised in the dim dear
    Beginnings of the year.
In these young days you meditate your part;
    I have it all by heart.
I know the secrets of the seeds of flowers
    Hidden and warm with showers,
And how, in kindling Spring, the cuckoo shall
    Alter his interval.
But not a flower or song I ponder is
    My own, but memory's.
I shall be silent in those days desired
    Before a world inspired.
O all brown birds, compose your old song-phrases,
    Earth, thy familiar daisies!

A poet mused upon the dusky height,
    Between two stars towards night,
His purpose in his heart. I watched, a space,
    The meaning of his face:

There was the secret, fled from earth and skies,
    Hid in his grey young eyes.
My heart and all the Summer wait his choice,
    And wonder for his voice.
Who shall foretell his songs, and who aspire
    But to divine his lyre?
Sweet earth, we know thy dimmest mysteries,
    But he is lord of his.

TO ANY POET

Thou who singest through the earth
All the earth's wild creatures fly thee;
Everywhere thou marrest mirth,—
    Dumbly they defy thee;
There is something they deny thee.

Pines thy fallen nature ever
For the unfallen Nature sweet.
But she shuns thy long endeavour,
    Though her flowers and wheat
Throng and press thy pausing feet.

Though thou tame a bird to love thee,
Press thy face to grass and flowers,
All these things reserve above thee
    Secrets in the bowers,
Secrets in the sun and showers.

Sing thy sorrow, sing thy gladness,
In thy songs must wind and tree
Bear the fictions of thy sadness,
    Thy humanity.
For their truth is not for thee.

Wait, and many a secret nest,
Many a hoarded winter-store
Will be hidden on thy breast.
    Things thou longest for
Will not fear or shun thee more.

Thou shalt intimately lie
In the roots of flowers that thrust
Upwards from thee to the sky,
    With no more distrust
When they blossom from thy dust.

Silent labours of the rain
Shall be near thee, reconciled;
Little lives of leaves and grain,
    All things shy and wild,
Tell thee secrets, quiet child.

Earth, set free from thy fair fancies
And the art thou shalt resign,
Will bring forth her rue and pansies
    Unto more divine
Thoughts than any thoughts of thine.

Nought will fear thee, humbled creature.
There will lie thy mortal burden
Pressed unto the heart of Nature,
    Songless in a garden,
With a long embrace of pardon.

Then the truth all creatures tell,
And His will Whom thou entreatest
Shall absorb thee; there shall dwell
    Silence, the completest
Of thy poems, last and sweetest.

BUILDERS OF RUINS

We build with strength the deep tower wall
   That shall be shattered thus and thus.
And fair and great are court and hall,
   But *how* fair—this is not for us,
Who know the lack that lurks in all.

We know, we know how all too bright
   The hues are that our painting wears,
And how the marble gleams too white;—
   We speak in unknown tongues, the years
Interpret everything aright,

And crown with weeds our pride of towers,
   And warm our marble through with sun,
And break our pavements through with flowers,
   With an Amen when all is done,
Knowing these perfect things of ours.

O days, we ponder, left alone,
   Like children in their lonely hour,
And in our secrets keep your own,
   As seeds the colour of the flower.
To-day they are not all unknown,

The stars that 'twixt the rise and fall,
   Like relic-seers, shall one by one
Stand musing o'er our empty hall;
   And setting moons shall brood upon
The frescoes of our inward wall.

And when some midsummer shall be,
   Hither will come some little one
(Dusty with bloom of flowers is he),
   Sit on a ruin i' the late long sun,
And think, one foot upon his knee.

And where they wrought, these lives of ours,
   So many-worded, many-souled,
A North-west wind will take the towers,
   And dark with colour, sunny and cold,
Will range alone among the flowers.

And here or there, at our desire,
   The little clamorous owl shall sit
Through her still time; and we aspire
   To make a law (and know not it)
Unto the life of a wild briar.

Our purpose is distinct and dear,
   Though from our open eyes 'tis hidden.
Thou, Time to come, shalt make it clear,
   Undoing our work; we are children chidden
With pity and smiles of many a year.

Who shall allot the praise, and guess
   What part is yours and what is ours?—
O years that certainly will bless
   Our flowers with fruits, our seeds with flowers,
With ruin all our perfectness.

Be patient, Time, of our delays,
   Too happy hopes, and wasted fears,
Our faithful ways, our wilful ways;
   Solace our labours, O our seers
The seasons, and our bards the days;

And make our pause and silence brim
　　With the shrill children's play, and sweets
Of those pathetic flowers and dim,
　　Of those eternal flowers my Keats,
Dying, felt growing over him!

THE LOVER URGES THE BETTER THRIFT

My Fair, no beauty of thine will last
   Save in my love's eternity.
   Thy smiles, that light thee fitfully,
Are lost for ever—their moment past—
   Except the few thou givest to me.

Thy sweet words vanish day by day,
   As all breath of mortality;
   Thy laughter, done, must cease to be,
And all thy dear tones pass away,
   Except the few that sing to me.

Hide then within my heart, O hide
   All thou art loth should go from thee.
   Be kinder to thyself and me.
My cupful from this river's tide
   Shall never reach the long sad sea.

SAN LORENZO'S MOTHER

I had not seen my son's dear face
(He chose the cloister by God's grace)
   Since it had come to full flower-time.
   I hardly guessed at its perfect prime,
That folded flower of his dear face.

Mine eyes were veiled by mists of tears
When on a day in many years
   One of his Order came. I thrilled,
   Facing, I thought, that face fulfilled.
I doubted, for my mists of tears.

His blessing be with me for ever!
My hope and doubt were hard to sever.
   —That altered face, those holy weeds.
   I filled his wallet and kissed his beads,
And lost his echoing feet for ever.

If to my son my alms were given
I know not, and I wait for Heaven.
   He did not plead for child of mine,
   But for another Child divine,
And unto Him it was surely given.

There is One alone who cannot change;
Dreams are we, shadows, visions strange;
   And all I give is given to One.
   I might mistake my dearest son,
But never the Son who cannot change.

TO A DAISY

Slight as thou art, thou art enough to hide
   Like all created things, secrets from me,
   And stand a barrier to eternity.
And I, how can I praise thee well and wide
From where I dwell—upon the hither side?
   Thou little veil for so great mystery,
   When shall I penetrate all things and thee,
And then look back? For this I must abide,

Till thou shalt grow and fold and be unfurled
Literally between me and the world.
   Then I shall drink from in beneath a spring,
And from a poet's side shall read his book.
O daisy mine, what will it be to look
   From God's side even of such a simple thing?

A DAY AND A LIFE

Clouds are mingled in changing grey:
A rainy morning in spring—so be it.
There'll be no revel of roses and may;
Go back—children who came to see it.
There'll be no noon on the hills to-day;

No deep sky lost in the sun, but rain;
No clouds like light in a light that is greater.
The young sky weeps in a youth of pain,
And though the sweet sun may send us later
Long glories over the level plain,

Yet there are slopes of Eastern lawn
Among the hills—those morning places,
With souls to the early time up-drawn;
With tremulous dews and dreamy faces
Set to the fresh thoughts of the dawn—

Set to the innocent airs, and sweet
Long sunshine of the morning only.
Though the fair plain of wood and wheat
Shine rainbow-robed, their shadows, lonely,
Will darken the country about their feet.

The sun may break: we will thank God for it,
In a long bright evening—who shall say?
The dark veil fall; but the morning wore it.
And many flowers will have done their day,
And many birds will have died before it.

RENOUNCEMENT

I must not think of thee; and, tired yet strong,
  I shun the thought that lurks in all delight—
  The thought of thee—and in the blue Heaven's height,
And in the sweetest passage of a song.
O just beyond the fairest thoughts that throng
  This breast, the thought of thee waits hidden yet bright;
  But it must never, never come in sight;
I must stop short of thee the whole day long.

But when sleep comes to close each difficult day,
  When night gives pause to the long watch I keep,
  And all my bonds I needs must loose apart,
Must doff my will as raiment laid away,—
  With the first dream that comes with the first sleep
  I run, I run, I am gathered to thy heart.

AFTER A PARTING

Farewell has long been said; I have foregone thee;
   I never name thee even.
But how shall I learn virtues and yet shun thee?
   For thou art so near Heaven
That Heavenward meditations pause upon thee.

Thou dost beset the path to every shrine;
   My trembling thoughts discern
Thy goodness in the good for which I pine;
   And, if I turn from but one sin, I turn
Unto a smile of thine.

How shall I thrust thee apart
   Since all my growth tends to thee night and day—
To thee faith, hope, and art?
   Swift are the currents setting all one way;
They draw my life, my life, out of my heart.

VENI CREATOR

So humble things Thou hast borne for us, O God,
Left'st Thou a path of lowliness untrod?
Yes, one, till now, another Olive-Garden.
For we endure the tender pain of pardon,—
One with another we forbear. Give heed,
Look at the mournful world Thou hast decreed.
The time has come. At last we hapless men
Know all our haplessness all through. Come, then,
Endure undreamed humility: Lord of Heaven,
Come to our ignorant hearts and be forgiven.

CRADLE-SONG AT TWILIGHT

The child not yet is lulled to rest.
   Too young a nurse, the slender Night
So laxly holds him to her breast
   That throbs with flight.

He plays with her, and will not sleep.
   For other playfellows she sighs;
An unmaternal fondness keep
   Her alien eyes.

PARENTAGE

'When Augustus Cæsar legislated against the unmarried citizens
of Rome, he declared them to be, in some sort, slayers of the people'.

    Ah! no, not these!
These, who were childless, are not they who gave
So many dead unto the journeying wave,
The helpless nurslings of the cradling seas;
Not they who doomed by infallible decrees
Unnumbered man to the innumerable grave.

    But those who slay
Are fathers. Theirs are armies. Death is theirs—
The death of innocences and despairs;
The dying of the golden and the grey.
The sentence, when these speak it, has no Nay.
And she who slays is she who bears, who bears.

THE LADY POVERTY

The Lady Poverty was fair:
But she has lost her looks of late,
With change of times and change of air.
Ah slattern! she neglects her hair,
Her gown, her shoes; she keeps no state
As once when her pure feet were bare.

Or—almost worse, if worse can be—
She scolds in parlours, dusts and trims,
Watches and counts. O is this she
Whom Francis met, whose step was free,
Who with Obedience carolled hymns,
In Umbria walked with Chastity?

Where is her ladyhood? Not here,
Not among modern kinds of men;
But in the stony fields, where clear
Through the thin trees the skies appear,
In delicate spare soil and fen,
And slender landscape and austere.

'I AM THE WAY'

Thou art the Way.
Hadst Thou been nothing but the goal,
      I cannot say
If Thou hadst ever met my soul.

      I cannot see—
I, child of process—if there lies
      An end for me,
Full of repose, full of replies.

      I'll not reproach
The road that winds, my feet that err.
      Access, Approach
Art Thou, Time, Way, and Wayfarer.

'You never attained to Him?' 'If to attain
    Be to abide, then that may be'.
'Endless the way, followed with how much pain!'
    'The way was He'.

NOVEMBER BLUE

The golden tint of the electric lights seems to give a complementary
colour to the air in the early evening.—ESSAY ON LONDON

O Heavenly colour, London town
    Has blurred it from her skies;
And, hooded in an earthly brown,
    Unheaven'd the city lies.
No longer, standard-like, this hue
    Above the broad road flies;
Nor does the narrow street the blue
    Wear, slender pennon-wise.

But when the gold and silver lamps
    Colour the London dew,
And, misted by the winter damps,
    The shops shine bright anew—
Blue comes to earth, it walks the street,
    It dyes the wide air through;
A mimic sky about their feet,
    The throng go crowned with blue.

THE MODERN MOTHER

Oh, what a kiss
With filial passion overcharged is this!
    To this misgiving breast
This child runs, as a child ne'er ran to rest
Upon the light heart and the unoppressed.

    Unhoped, unsought!
A little tenderness, this mother thought
    The utmost of her meed.
She looked for gratitude; content indeed
With thus much that her nine years' love had bought.

    Nay, even with less.
This mother, giver of life, death, peace, distress,
    Desired ah! not so much
Thanks as forgiveness; and the passing touch
Expected, and the slight, the brief caress.

    O filial light
Strong in these childish eyes, these new, these bright
    Intelligible stars! Their rays
Are near the constant earth, guides in the maze,
Natural, true, keen in this dusk of days.

MATERNITY

One wept whose only child was dead,
    New-born, ten years ago.
'Weep not; he is in bliss,' they said.
    She answered, 'Even so,

'Ten years ago was born in pain
    A child, not now forlorn.
But oh, ten years ago, in vain,
    A mother, a mother was born'.

THE RAINY SUMMER

There's much afoot in heaven and earth this year;
   The winds hunt up the sun, hunt up the moon,
Trouble the dubious dawn, hasten the drear
   Height of a threatening noon.

No breath of boughs, no breath of leaves, of fronds,
   May linger or grow warm; the trees are loud;
The forest, rooted, tosses in her bonds,
   And strains against the cloud.

No scents may pause within the garden-fold;
   The rifled flowers are cold as ocean-shells;
Bees, humming in the storm, carry their cold
   Wild honey to cold cells.

TO THE BODY

Thou inmost, ultimate
Council of judgement, palace of decrees,
Where the high senses hold their spiritual state,
    Sued by earth's embassies,
And sign, approve, accept, conceive, create;

    Create—thy senses close
With the world's pleas. The random odours reach
Their sweetness in the place of thy repose,
    Upon thy tongue the peach,
And in thy nostrils breathes the breathing rose.

    To thee, secluded one,
The dark vibrations of the sightless skies,
The lovely inexplicit colours, run;
    The light gropes for those eyes.
O thou august! thou dost command the sun.

    Music, all dumb, hath trod
Into thine ear her one effectual way;
And fire and cold approach to gain thy nod,
    Where thou call'st up the day,
Where thou awaitest the appeal of God.

A GENERAL COMMUNION

I saw the throng, so deeply separate,
    Fed at one only board—
The devout people, moved, intent, elate,
    And the devoted Lord.

O struck apart! not side from human side,
    But soul from human soul,
As each asunder absorbed the multiplied,
    The ever unparted, whole.

I saw this people as a field of flowers,
    Each grown at such a price
The sum of unimaginable powers
    Did no more than suffice.

A thousand single central daisies they,
    A thousand of the one;
For each, the entire monopoly of day;
    For each, the whole of the devoted sun.

IN PORTUGAL, 1912

And will they cast the altars down,
    Scatter the chalice, crush the bread?
In field, in village, and in town
    He hides an unregarded head;

Waits in the corn-lands far and near,
    Bright in His sun, dark in His frost,
Sweet in the vine, ripe in the ear—
    Lonely unconsecrated Host.

In ambush at the merry board
    The Victim lurks unsacrificed;
The mill conceals the harvest's Lord,
    The wine-press holds the unbidden Christ.

IN MANCHESTER SQUARE

In Memoriam T. H.

The paralytic man has dropped in death
    The crossing-sweeper's brush to which he clung,
One-handed, twisted, dwarfed, scanted of breath,
    Although his hair was young.

I saw this year the winter vines of France,
    Dwarfed, twisted goblins in the frosty drouth—
Gnarled, crippled, blackened little stems askance
    On long hills to the South.

Great green and golden hands of leaves ere long
    Shall proffer clusters in that vineyard wide.
And O his might, his sweet, his wine, his song,
    His stature, since he died!

THE LAUNCH

Forth, to the alien gravity,
Forth, to the laws of ocean, we,
    Builders on earth by laws of land,
    Entrust this creature of our hand
Upon the calculated sea.

Fast bound to shore we cling, we creep,
And make our ship ready to leap
    Light to the flood, equipped to ride
    The strange conditions of the tide—
New weight, new force, new world: the Deep.

Ah thus—not thus—the Dying, kissed,
Cherished, exhorted, shriven, dismissed;
    By all the eager means we hold
    We, warm, prepare him for the cold,
To keep the incalculable tryst.

EASTER NIGHT

All night had shout of men and cry
    Of woeful women filled His way;
Until that noon of sombre sky
    On Friday, clamour and display
Smote Him; no solitude had He,
No silence, since Gethsemane.

Public was Death; but Power, but Might,
    But Life again, but Victory,
Were hushed within the dead of night,
    The shutter'd dark, the secrecy.
And all alone, alone, alone,
He rose again behind the stone.

TO O——, OF HER DARK EYES

Across what calm of tropic seas,
   'Neath alien clusters of the nights,
Looked, in the past, such eyes as these?
   Long-quenched, relumed, ancestral lights!

The generations fostered them;
   And steadfast Nature, secretwise—
Thou seedling child of that old stem—
   Kindled anew thy dark-bright eyes.

Was it a century or two
   This lovely darkness rose and set,
Occluded by grey eyes and blue,
   And Nature feigning to forget?

Some grandam gave a hint of it—
   So cherished was it in thy race,
So fine a treasure to transmit
   In its perfection to thy face.

Some father to some mother's breast
   Entrusted it, unknowing. Time
Implied, or made it manifest,
   Bequest of a forgotten clime.

Hereditary eyes! But this
   Is single, singular, apart:—
New-made thy love, new-made thy kiss,
   New-made thy errand to my heart.

THE TWO SHAKESPEARE TERCENTENARIES

OF BIRTH, 1864; OF DEATH, 1916

To Shakespeare

Longer than thine, than thine,
Is now my time of life; and thus thy years
Seem to be clasped and harboured within mine.
O how ignoble this my clasp appears!

Thy unprophetic birth,
Thy darkling death: living I might have seen
That cradle, marked those labours, closed that earth.
O first, O last, O infinite between!

Now that my life has shared
Thy dedicated date, O mortal, twice,
To what all-vain embrace shall be compared
My lean enclosure of thy paradise:

To ignorant arms that fold
A poet to a foolish breast? The Line,
That is not, with the world within its hold?
So, days with days, my days encompass thine.

Child, Stripling, Man—the sod.
Might I talk little language to thee, pore
On thy last silence? O thou city of God,
My waste lies after thee, and lies before.

'A riddling world!' one cried.
'If pangs must be, would God that they were sent
To the impure, the cruel, and passed aside
 The holy innocent!'

But I, 'Ah no, no, no!
Not the clean heart transpierced; not tears that fall
For a child's agony; nor a martyr's woe;
 Not these, not these appal.

'Not docile motherhood,
Dutiful, frequent, closed in all distress;
Not shedding of the unoffending blood;
 Not little joy grown less;

'Not all-benign old age
With dotage mocked; not gallantry that faints
And still pursues; not the vile heritage
 Of sin's disease in saints;

'Not these defeat the mind.
For great is that abjection, and august
That irony. Submissive we shall find
 A splendour in that dust.

'Not these puzzle the will;
Not these the yet unanswered question urge.
But the unjust stricken; but the hands that kill
 Lopped; but the merited scourge;

'The sensualist at fast;
The merciless felled; the liar in his snares.
The cowardice of my judgment sees, aghast,
    The flail, the chaff, the tares'.

INTIMATIONS OF MORTALITY

From Recollections of Early Childhood

> A simple child . . .
>   That lightly draws its breath
> And feels its life in every limb,
>   What should it know of death?
>   WORDSWORTH

It knows but will not tell.
    Awake, alone, it counts its father's years—
How few are left—its mother's. Ah, how well
    It knows of death, in tears.

If any of the three—
    Parents and child—believe they have prevailed
To keep the secret of mortality,
    I know that two have failed.

The third, the lonely, keeps
    One secret—a child's knowledge. When they come
At night to ask wherefore the sweet one weeps,
    Those hidden lips are dumb.

THE THRESHING-MACHINE

No 'fan is in his hand' for these
Young villagers beneath the trees,
   Watching the wheels. But I recall
   The rhythm of rods that rise and fall,
Purging the harvest, over-seas.

No fan, no flail, no threshing-floor!
And all their symbols evermore
   Forgone in England now—the sign,
   The visible pledge, the threat divine,
The chaff dispersed, the wheat in store.

The unbreathing engine marks no tune,
Steady at sunrise, steady at noon,
   Inhuman, perfect, saving time,
   And saving measure, and saving rhyme—
And did our Ruskin speak too soon?

'No noble strength on earth' he sees
'Save Hercules' arm'; his grave decrees
   Curse wheel and steam. As the wheels ran
   I saw the other strength of man,
I knew the brain of Hercules.

TO 'A CERTAIN RICH MAN'

*'I have five brethren. . . . Father, I beseech thee . . . lest they come to
this place'* ——ST. LUKE'S GOSPEL

Thou wouldst not part thy spoil
Gained from the beggar's want, the weakling's toil,
Nor spare a jot of sumptuousness or state
For Lazarus at the gate.

And in the appalling night
Of expiation, as in day's delight,
Thou heldst thy niggard hand; it would not share
One hour of thy despair.

Those five—thy prayer for them!
O generous! who, condemned, wouldst not condemn,
Whose ultimate human greatness proved thee so
A miser of thy woe.

'LORD, I OWE THEE A DEATH'

In Time of War— RICHARD HOOKER

Man pays that debt with new munificence,
    Not piecemeal now, not slowly, by the old:
Not grudgingly, by the effaced thin pence,
    But greatly and in gold.

'RIVERS UNKNOWN TO SONG'

—JAMES THOMSON

Wide waters in the waste; or, out of reach,
   Rough Alpine falls where late a glacier hung;
Or rivers groping for the alien beach,
   Through continents, unsung.

Nay, not these nameless, these remote, alone;
   But all the streams from all the watersheds—
Peneus, Danube, Nile—are the unknown
   Young in their ancient beds.

Man has no tale for them. O travellers swift
   From secrets to oblivion! Waters wild
That pass in act to bend a flower, or lift
   The bright limbs of a child!

For they are new, they are fresh; there's no surprise
   Like theirs on earth. O strange for evermore!
This moment's Tiber with his shining eyes
   Never saw Rome before.

Man has no word for their eternity—
   Rhine, Avon, Arno, younglings, youth uncrowned:
Ignorant, innocent, instantaneous, free,
   Unwelcomed, unrenowned.

TO ANTIQUITY

. . . Reverence for our fathers, with their stores of experiences
—AN AUTHOR WHOSE NAME I DID NOT NOTE

O our young ancestor,
   Our boy in Letters, how we trudge oppressed
With our 'experiences,' and you of yore
   Flew light, and blessed!

Youngling, in your new town,
   Tight, like a box of toys—the town that is
Our shattered, open ruin, with its crown
   Of histories;

You with your morning words
   Fresh from the night, your yet un-sonneted moon;
Your passion undismayed, cool as a bird's
   Ignorant tune;

O youngling! how is this?
   Your poems are not wearied yet, not dead.
Must I bow low? or, with an envious kiss,
   Put you to bed?

TO SLEEP

Dear fool, be true to me!
I know the poets speak thee fair, and I
Hail thee uncivilly.
O but I call with a more urgent cry!

I do not prize thee less,
I need thee more, that thou dost love to teach—
Father of foolishness—
The imbecile dreams clear out of wisdom's reach.

Come and release me; bring
My irresponsible mind; come in thy hours;
Draw from my soul the sting
Of wit that trembles, consciousness that cowers.

For if night comes without thee
She is more cruel than day. But thou, fulfil
Thy work, thy gifts about thee—
Liberty, liberty, from this weight of will.

My day-mind can endure
Upright, in hope, all it must undergo.
But O afraid, unsure,
My night-mind waking lies too low, too low.

Dear fool, be true to me!
The night is thine, man yields it, it beseems
Thy ironic dignity.
Make me all night the innocent fool that dreams.

A COMPARISON IN A SEASIDE FIELD

'Tis royal and authentic June
    Over this poor soil blossoming;
Here lies, beneath an upright noon,
    Thin nation for so wild a king.

Far off, the noble Summer rules,
    Violent in the ardent rose,
His sun alight in mirroring pools,
    Braggart on Alps of vanquished snows;

Away, aloft, true to his hour,
    Announced, his colour, his fire, his jest.
But here, in negligible flower,
    Summer is not proclaimed:—confessed.

A woman I marked; for her no state,
    Small joy, no song. She had her boon,
Her only youth, true to its date,
    Faintly perceptible, her June.

WINTER TREES ON THE HORIZON

O delicate! Even in wooded lands
　They show the margin of my world,
My own horizon; little bands
　Of twigs unveil that edge impearled.

And what is more mine own than this—
　My limit, level with mine eyes?
For me precisely do they kiss—
　The rounded earth, the rounding skies.

It has my stature, that keen line
　(Let mathematics vouch for it).
The lark's horizon is not mine,
　No, nor his nestlings' where they sit;

No, nor the child's. And, when I gain
　The hills, I lift it as I rise
Erect; anon, back to the plain
　I soothe it with mine equal eyes.

Dear laws, come to my breast!
Take all my frame, and make your close arms meet
Around me; and so ruled, so warmed, so pressed,
I breathe, aware; I feel my wild heart beat.

Dear laws, be wings to me!
The feather merely floats. O be it heard
Through weight of life—the skylark's gravity—
That I am not a feather, but a bird.

PART II

ESSAYS

If life is not always poetical, it is at least metrical. Periodicity rules over the mental experience of man, according to the path of the orbit of his thoughts. Distances are not gauged, ellipses not measured, velocities not ascertained, times not known. Nevertheless, the recurrence is sure. What the mind suffered last week, or last year, it does not suffer now; but it will suffer again next week or next year. Happiness is not a matter of events; it depends upon the tides of the mind. Disease is metrical, closing in at shorter and shorter periods towards death, sweeping abroad at longer and longer intervals towards recovery. Sorrow for one cause was intolerable yesterday, and will be intolerable to-morrow; to-day it is easy to bear, but the cause has not passed. Even the burden of a spiritual distress unsolved is bound to leave the heart to a temporary peace; and remorse itself does not remain—it returns. Gaiety takes us by a dear surprise. If we had made a course of notes of its visits, we might have been on the watch, and would have had an expectation instead of a discovery. No one makes such observations; in all the diaries of students of the interior world, there have never come to light the records of the Kepler of such cycles. But Thomas à Kempis knew of the recurrences, if he did not measure them. In his cell alone with the elements— 'What wouldst thou more than these? for out of these were all things made'—he learnt the stay to be found in the depth of the hour of bitterness, and the remembrance that restrains the soul at the coming of the moment of delight, giving it a more conscious welcome, but presaging for it an inexorable flight. And 'rarely, rarely comest thou,' sighed Shelley, not to Delight merely, but to the Spirit of Delight. Delight can be compelled beforehand, called, and constrained to our service—Ariel can be bound to a daily task; but such artificial violence throws life out of metre, and it is not the spirit that is thus compelled. *That* flits upon an orbit elliptically or parabolically or hyperbolically curved, keeping no man knows what trysts with Time.

It seems fit that Shelley and the author of the 'Imitation' should both have been keen and simple enough to perceive these flights, and to guess at the order of this periodicity. Both souls were in close touch with the spirits of their several worlds, and no deliberate human rules, no infractions of the liberty and law of the universal movement, kept from them the knowledge of recurrences. *Eppur si muove*. They knew that presence does not exist without absence; they knew that what is just upon its flight of farewell is already on its long path of return. They knew that what is approaching to the very touch is hastening towards departure. 'O wind,' cried Shelley, in autumn,

O wind,
If winter comes can spring be far behind?

They knew that the flux is equal to the reflux; that to interrupt with unlawful recurrences, out of time, is to weaken the impulse of onset and retreat; the sweep and impetus of movement. To live in constant efforts after an equal life, whether the equality be sought in mental production, or in spiritual sweetness, or in the joy of the senses, is to live without either rest or full activity. The souls of certain of the saints, being singularly simple and single, have been in the most complete subjection to the law of periodicity. Ecstasy and desolation visited them by seasons. They endured, during spaces of vacant time, the interior loss of all for which they had sacrificed the world. They rejoiced in the uncovenanted beatitude of sweetness alighting in their hearts. Like them are the poets whom, three times or ten times in the course of a long life, the Muse has approached, touched, and forsaken. And yet hardly like them; not always so docile, nor so wholly prepared for the departure, the brevity, of the golden and irrevocable hour. Few poets have fully recognized the metrical absence of their Muse. For full recognition is expressed in one only way—silence.

It has been found that several tribes in Africa and in America worship the moon, and not the sun; a great number worship both; but no tribes are known to adore the sun, and not the moon. On her depend the tides; and she is Selene, mother of Herse, bringer of the dews that recurrently irrigate lands where rain is rare. More than any other companion of earth is she the Measurer. Early Indo-Germanic languages knew her by that name. Her metrical phases are the symbol of the order of recurrence. Constancy in approach and in departure is the reason of her inconstancies. Juliet will not receive a vow spoken in invocation of the moon; but Juliet did not live to know that love itself has tidal times—lapses and ebbs which are due to the metrical rule of the interior heart, but which the lover vainly and unkindly attributes to some outward alteration in the beloved. For man—except those elect already named—is hardly aware of periodicity. The individual man either never learns it fully, or learns it late. And he learns it so late, because it is a matter of cumulative experience upon which cumulative evidence is long lacking. It is in the after-part of each life that the law is learnt so definitely as to do away with the hope or fear of continuance. That young sorrow comes so near to despair is a result of this young ignorance. So is the early hope of great achievement. Life seems so long, and its capacity so great, to one who knows nothing of all the intervals it needs must hold—intervals between aspirations, between actions, pauses as inevitable as the pauses of sleep. And life looks impossible to the young unfortunate, unaware of the inevitable and unfailing refreshment. It would be for their peace to learn that there is a tide in the affairs of men, in a sense more subtle—if it is not too audacious to add a meaning to Shakespeare—than the phrase was meant to contain. Their joy is flying away from them on its way home; their life will wax and wane; and if they would be wise, they must wake and rest in its phases, knowing that they are ruled by the law that commands all things—a sun's revolutions and the rhythmic pangs of maternity.

The mothers of Professors were indulged in the practice of jumping at conclusions, and were praised for their impatience of the slow process of reason.

Professors have written of the mental habits of women as though they accumulated generation by generation upon women, and passed over their sons. Professors take it for granted, obviously by some process other than the slow process of reason, that women derive from their mothers and grandmothers, and men from their fathers and grandfathers. This, for instance, was written lately: 'This power [it matters not what] would be about equal in the two sexes but for the influence of heredity, which turns the scale in favour of the woman, as for long generations the surroundings and conditions of life of the female sex have developed in her a greater degree of the power in question than circumstances have required from men'. 'Long generations' of subjection are, strangely enough, held to excuse the timorousness and the shifts of women to-day. But the world, unknowing, tampers with the courage of its sons by such a slovenly indulgence. It tampers with their intelligence by fostering the ignorance of women.

And yet Shakespeare confessed the participation of man and woman in their common heritage. It is Cassius who speaks:

> Have you not love enough to bear with me
> When that rash humour which my mother gave me
> Makes me forgetful?

And Brutus who replies:

> Yes, Cassius, and from henceforth
> When you are over-earnest with your Brutus
> He'll think your mother chides, and leave you so.

Dryden confessed it also in his praises of Anne Killigrew:

> If by traduction came thy mind,
> Our wonder is the less to find
> A soul so charming from a stock so good.
> Thy father was transfused into thy blood.

The winning of Waterloo upon the Eton playgrounds is very well; but there have been some other, and happily minor, fields that were not won—that were more or less lost. Where did this loss take place, if the gains were secured at football? This inquiry is not quite so cheerful as the other. But while the victories were once going forward in the playground, the defeats or disasters were once going forward in some other place, presumably. And this was surely the place that was not a playground, the place where the future wives of the football players were sitting still while their future husbands were playing football.

This is the train of thought that followed the grey figure of a woman on a bicycle in Oxford Street. She had an enormous and top-heavy omnibus at her back. All the things on the near side of the street—the things going her way—were going at different paces, in two streams, overtaking and being overtaken. The tributary streets shot omnibuses and carriages, cabs and carts—some to go her own way, some with an impetus that carried them curving into the other current, and other some making a straight line right across Oxford Street into the street opposite. Besides all the unequal movement, there were the stoppings. It was a delicate tangle to keep from knotting. The nerves of the mouths of horses bore the whole charge and answered it, as they do every day.

The woman in grey, quite alone, was immediately dependent on no nerves but her own, which almost made her machine sensitive. But this alertness was joined to such perfect composure as no flutter of a moment disturbed. There was the steadiness of sleep, and a vigilance more than that of an ordinary waking.

At the same time, the woman was doing what nothing in her youth could well have prepared her for. She must have passed a childhood unlike the ordinary girl's childhood, if her steadiness or her alertness had ever been educated, if she had been rebuked for cowardice, for the egoistic distrust of general rules, or for claims of exceptional chances. Yet here she was, trusting not only herself but a multitude of other people; taking her equal risk; giving a watchful confidence to averages—that last, perhaps, her strangest and greatest success.

No exceptions were hers, no appeals, and no forewarnings. She evidently had not in her mind a single phrase, familiar to women, made to express no confidence except in accidents, and to proclaim a prudent foresight of the less probable event. No woman could ride a bicycle along Oxford Street with any such baggage as that about her.

The woman in grey had a watchful confidence not only in a multitude of men but in a multitude of things. And it is very hard for any untrained human being to practise confidence in things in motion—things full of force, and, what is worse, of forces. Moreover, there is a supreme difficulty for a mind accustomed to search timorously for some little place of insignificant rest on any accessible point of stable equilibrium; and that is the difficulty of holding itself nimbly secure in an equilibrium that is unstable. Who can deny that women are generally used to look about for the little stationary repose just described? Whether in intellectual or in spiritual things, they do not often live without it.

She, none the less, fled upon unstable equilibrium, escaped upon it, depended upon it, trusted it, was 'ware of it, was on guard against it, as she sped amid her crowd her own unstable equilibrium, her machine's, that of the judgment, the temper, the skill, the perception, the strength of men and horses.

She had learnt the difficult peace of suspense. She had learnt also the lowly and self-denying faith in common chances. She had learnt to be content with her share—no more—in common security, and to be pleased with her part in common hope. For all this, it may be repeated, she could have had but small preparation. Yet no anxiety was hers, no uneasy distrust and disbelief of that human thing—an average of life and death.

To this courage the woman in grey had attained with a spring, and she had seated herself suddenly upon a place of detachment between earth and air, freed from the principal detentions, weights, and embarrassments of the usual life of fear. She had made herself, as it were, light, so as not to dwell either in security or danger, but to pass between them. She confessed difficulty and peril by her delicate evasions, and consented to rest in neither. She would not owe safety to the mere motionlessness of a seat on the solid earth, but she used gravitation to balance the slight burdens of her wariness and her confidence. She put aside all the pride and vanity of terror, and leapt into an unsure condition of liberty and content.

She leapt, too, into a life of moments. No pause was possible to her as she went, except the vibrating pause of a perpetual change and of an unflagging flight. A woman, long educated to sit still, does not suddenly learn to live a momentary life without strong momentary resolution. She has no light achievement in limiting not only her foresight, which must become brief, but her memory, which must do more; for it must rather cease than become brief. Idle memory wastes time and other things. The moments of the woman in grey as they dropped by must needs disappear, and be simply forgotten, as a child forgets. Idle memory, by the way, shortens life, or shortens the sense of time, by linking the immediate past clingingly to the present. Here may possibly be found one of the reasons for the length of a child's time, and for the brevity of the time that succeeds. The child lets his moments pass by and quickly become remote through a thousand little successive oblivions. He has not yet the languid habit of recall. 'Thou art my warrior,' said Volumnia. 'I holp to frame thee'.

Shall a man inherit his mother's trick of speaking, or her habit and attitude, and not suffer something, against his will, from her bequest of weakness, and something, against his heart, from her bequest of folly? From the legacies of an unlessoned mind, a woman's heirs-male are not cut off in the Common Law of the generations of mankind. Brutus knew that the valour of Portia was settled upon his sons.

Through the long history of human relations, which is the history of the life of our race, there sounds at intervals the clamour of a single voice which has not the tone of oratory, but asks, answers, interrupts itself, interrupts—what else? Whatever else it interrupts is silence; there are pauses, but no answers. There is the jest without the laugh, and again the laugh without the jest. And this is because the letters written by Madame de Sévigné were all saved, and not many written to her; because Swift burnt the letters that were the dearest things in life to him, while 'MD' both made a treasury of his; and because Prue kept all the letters which Steele wrote to her from their marriage-day onwards, and Steele kept none of hers.

In Swift's case the silence is full of echoes; that is to say, his letters repeat the phrases of Stella's and Dingley's, to play with them, flout them, and toss them back against the two silenced voices. He never lets the word of these two women fall to the ground; and when they have but blundered with it, and aimed it wide, and sent it weakly, he will catch it, and play you twenty delicate and expert juggling pranks with it as he sends it back into their innocent faces. So we have something of MD's letters in the 'Journal,' and this in the only form in which we desire them, to tell the truth; for when Swift gravely saves us some specimens of Stella's wit, after her death, as she spoke them, and not as he mimicked them, they make a sorry show.

In many correspondences, where one voice remains and the other is gone, the retort is enough for two. It is as when, the other day, the half of a pretty quarrel between nurse and child came down from an upper floor to the ears of a mother who decided that she need not interfere. The voice of the undaunted child it was that was audible alone, and it replied,

'I'm not; *you* are'; and anon, 'I'll tell *yours*'. Nothing was really missing there.

But Steele's letters to Prue, his wife, are no such simple matter. The turn we shall give them depends upon the unheard tone whereto they reply. And there is room for conjecture. It has pleased the more modern of the many spirits of banter to supply Prue's eternal silence with the voice of a scold. It is painful to me to complain of Thackeray; but see what a figure he makes of Prue in 'Esmond'. It is, says the nineteenth-century humourist, in defence against the pursuit of a jealous, exacting, neglected, or evaded wife that poor Dick Steele sends those little notes of excuse: 'Dearest Being on earth, pardon me if you do not see me till eleven o'clock, having met a schoolfellow from India'; 'My dear, dear wife, I write to let you know I do not come home to dinner, being obliged to attend some business abroad, of which I shall give you an account (when I see you in the evening), as becomes your dutiful and obedient husband'; 'Dear Prue, I cannot come home to dinner. I languish for your welfare'; 'I stay here in order to get Tonson to discount a bill for me, and shall dine with him to that end'; and so forth. Once only does Steele really afford the recent humourist the suggestion that is apparently always so welcome. It is when he writes that he is invited to supper to Mr. Boyle's, and adds: 'Dear Prue, do not send after me, for I shall be ridiculous'. But even this is to be read not ungracefully by a well-graced reader. Prue was young and unused to the world. Her husband, by the way, had been already married; and his greater age makes his constant deference all the more charming.

But with this one exception, Steele's little notes, kept by his wife while she lived, and treasured after her death by her daughter and his, are no record of the watchings and dodgings of a London farce. It is worth while to remember that Steele's dinner, which it was so often difficult to eat at home, was a thing of midday, and therefore of mid-business. But that is a detail. What is desirable is that a reasonable degree of sweetness should be attributed to Prue; for it is no more than just. To her Steele wrote in a dedication: 'How often has your tenderness removed pain from my aching head, how often anguish from my afflicted heart. If there are such beings as guardian angels, they are thus employed. I cannot believe one of them to be more good in inclination, or more charming in form, than my wife'.

True, this was for the public; but not so were these daily notes; and these carry to her his assurance that she is 'the beautifullest object in the world. I know no happiness in this life in any degree comparable to the pleasure I have in your person and society'. 'But indeed, though you have every perfection, you have an extravagant fault, which almost frustrates the good in you to me; and that is, that you do not love to dress, to appear, to shine out, even at my request, and to make me proud of you, or rather to indulge the pride I have that you are mine'. The correction of the phrase is finely considerate.

Prue cannot have been a dull wife, for this last compliment is a reply, full of polite alacrity, to a letter from her asking for a little flattery. How assiduously, and with what a civilized absence of uncouthness, of shame-facedness, and of slang of the mind, with what simplicity, alertness, and finish, does he step out at her invitation, and perform! She wanted a compliment, though they had been long married then, and he immediately turned it. This was no dowdy Prue.

Her request, by the way, which he repeats in obeying it, is one of the few instances of the other side of the correspondence—one of the few direct echoes of that one of the two voices which is silent.

The ceremony of the letters and the deferent method of address and signature are never dropped in this most intimate of letter-writing. It is not a little depressing to think that in this very form and state is supposed, by the modern reader, to lurk the stealthiness of the husband of farce, the 'rogue'. One does not like the word. Is it not clownish to apply it with intention to the husband of Prue? He did not pay, he was always in difficulties, he hid from bailiffs, he did many other things that tarnish honour, more or less, and things for which he had to beg Prue's special pardon; but yet he is not a fit subject for the unhandsome incredulity which is proud to be always at hand with an ironic commentary on such letters as his.

I have no wish to bowdlerize Sir Richard Steele, his ways and words. He wrote to Prue at night when the burgundy had been too much for him, and in the morning after. He announces that he is coming to her 'within a pint of wine'. One of his gayest letters—a love-letter before the marriage, addressed to 'dear lovely Mrs. Scurlock'—confesses candidly that he had been pledging her too well: 'I have been in very good company, where your health, under the character of the woman I loved best, has been often drunk; so that I may say that I am dead drunk for your sake, which is more than *I die for you*'.

Steele obviously drank burgundy wildly, as did his 'good company'; as did also the admirable Addison, who was so solitary in character and so serene in temperament. But no one has, for this fault, the right to put a railing accusation into the mouth of Prue. Every woman has a right to her own silence, whether her silence be hers of set purpose or by accident. And every creature has a right to security from the banterings peculiar to the humourists of a succeeding age. To every century its own ironies, to every century its own vulgarities. In Steele's time they had theirs. They might have rallied Prue more coarsely, but it would have been with a different rallying. Writers of the nineteenth century went about to rob her of her grace.

She kept some four hundred of these little letters of her lord's. It was a loyal keeping. But what does Thackeray call it? His word is 'thrifty'. He says: 'There are four hundred letters of Dick Steele's to his wife, which that thrifty woman preserved accurately'.

'Thrifty' is a hard word to apply to her whom Steele styled, in the year before her death, his 'charming little insolent'. She was ill in Wales, and he, at home, wept upon her pillow, and 'took it to be a sin to go to sleep'. Thrifty they may call her, and accurate if they will; but she lies in Westminster Abbey, and Steele called her 'your Prueship'.

This paper shall not be headed 'Tetty'. What may be a graceful enough freedom with the wives of other men shall be prohibited in the case of Johnson's, she with whose name no writer until now has scrupled to take freedoms whereto all graces were lacking. 'Tetty' it should not be, if for no other reason, for this—that the chance of writing 'Tetty' as a title is a kind of facile literary opportunity; it shall be denied. The Essay owes thus much amends of deliberate care to Dr. Johnson's wife. But, indeed, the reason is graver. What wish would he have had but that the language in the making whereof he took no ignoble part should somewhere, at some time, treat his only friend with ordinary honour?

Men who would trust Dr. Johnson with their orthodoxy, with their vocabulary, and with the most intimate vanity of their human wishes, refuse, with every mark of insolence, to trust him in regard to his wife. On that one point no reverence is paid to him, no deference, no respect, not so much as the credit due to our common sanity. Yet he is not reviled on account of his Thrale—nor, indeed, is his Thrale now seriously reproached for her Piozzi. It is true that Macaulay, preparing himself and his reader 'in his well-known way' (as a rustic of Mr. Hardy's might have it) for the recital of her second marriage, says that it would have been well if she had been laid beside the kind and generous Thrale when, in the prime of her life, he died. But Macaulay has not left us heirs to his indignation. His well-known way was to exhaust those possibilities of effect in which the commonplace is so rich. And he was permitted to point his paragraphs as he would, not only by calling Mrs. Thrale's attachment to her second husband 'a degrading passion,' but by summoning a chorus of 'all London' to the same purpose. She fled, he tells us, from the laughter and hisses of her countrymen and countrywomen to a land where she was unknown. Thus when Macaulay chastises Mrs. Elizabeth Porter for marrying Johnson, he is not inconsistent, for he pursues Mrs. Thrale with equal rigour for her audacity in keeping gaiety and grace in her mind and manners longer than Macaulay liked to see such ornaments added to the charm of twice 'married brows'.

It is not so with succeeding essayists. One of these minor biographers is so gentle as to call the attachment of Mrs. Thrale and Piozzi 'a mutual affection'. He adds, 'No one who has had some experience of life will be inclined to condemn Mrs. Thrale'. But there is no such courtesy, even from him, for Mrs. Johnson. Neither to him nor to any other writer has it yet occurred that if England loves her great Englishman's memory, she owes not only courtesy, but gratitude, to the only woman who loved him while there was yet time.

Not a thought of that debt has stayed the alacrity with which a caricature has been acclaimed as the only possible portrait of Mrs. Johnson. Garrick's school reminiscences would probably have made a much more charming woman grotesque. Garrick is welcome to his remembrances; we may even reserve for ourselves the liberty of envying those who heard him. But honest laughter should not fall into that tone of common antithesis which seems to say, 'See what are the absurdities of the great! Such is life! On this one point we, even we, are wiser than Dr. Johnson—we know how grotesque was his wife. We know something of the privacies of her toilet-table. We are able to compare her figure with the figures we, unlike him in his youth, have had the opportunity of admiring—the figures of the well-bred and well-dressed'. It is a sorry success to be able to say so much.

But in fact such a triumph belongs to no man. When Samuel Johnson, at twenty-six, married his wife, he gave the dull an advantage over himself which none but the dullest will take. He chose, for love, a woman who had the wit to admire him at first meeting, and in spite of first sight. 'That,' she said to her daughter, 'is the most sensible man I ever met'. He was penniless. She had what was no mean portion for those times and those conditions; and, granted that she was affected, and provincial, and short, and all the rest with which she is charged, she was probably not without suitors; nor do her defects or faults seem to have been those of an unadmired or neglected woman. Next, let us remember what was the aspect of Johnson's form and face, even in his twenties, and how little he could have touched the senses of a widow fond of externals. This one loved him, accepted him, made him happy, gave to one of the noblest of all English hearts the one love of its sombre life. And English literature has had no better phrase for her than Macaulay's—'She accepted, with a readiness which did her little honour, the addresses of a suitor who might have been her son'.

Her readiness did her incalculable honour. But it is at last worth remembering that Johnson had first done her incalculable honour. No one has given to man or woman the right to judge as to the worthiness of her who received it. The meanest man is generally allowed his own counsel as to his own wife; one of the greatest of men has been denied it. 'The lover,' says Macaulay, 'continued to be under the illusions of the wedding day till the lady died'. What is so graciously said is not enough. He was under those 'illusions' until he too died, when he had long passed her latest age, and was therefore able to set right that balance of years which has so much irritated the impertinent. Johnson passed from this life twelve years older than she, and so for twelve years his constant eyes had to turn backwards to dwell upon her. Time gave him a younger wife.

And here I will put into Mrs. Johnson's mouth, that mouth to which no one else has ever attributed any beautiful sayings, the words of Marceline Desbordes-Valmore to the young husband she loved: 'Older than thou! Let me never see thou knowest it. Forget it! I will remember it, to die before thy death'.

Macaulay, in his unerring effectiveness, uses Johnson's short sight for an added affront to Mrs. Johnson. The bridegroom was too weak of eyesight 'to distinguish ceruse from natural bloom'. Nevertheless, he saw well enough, when he was old, to distinguish Mrs. Thrale's dresses. He reproved her for wearing a dark dress; it was unsuitable, he said, for her size; a little creature should show gay colours 'like an insect'. We are not called upon to admire his wife; why, then, our taste being thus uncompromised, do we not suffer him to admire her? It is the most gratuitous kind of intrusion. Moreover, the biographers are eager to permit that touch of romance and grace in his relations to Mrs. Thrale, which they officially deny in the case of Mrs. Johnson. But the difference is all on the other side. He would not have bidden his wife dress like an insect. Mrs. Thrale was to him 'the first of womankind' only because his wife was dead.

Beauclerc, we learn, was wont to cap Garrick's mimicry of Johnson's love-making by repeating the words of Johnson himself in after-years—'It was a love-match on both sides'. And obviously he was as strange a lover as they said. Who doubted it? Was there any other woman in England to give such a suitor the opportunity of an eternal love? 'A life radically wretched,' was the life of this master of Letters; but she, who has received nothing in return except ignominy from these unthankful Letters, had been alone to make it otherwise. Well for him that he married so young as to earn the ridicule of all the biographers in England; for by doing so he, most happily, possessed his wife for nearly twenty years. I have called her his only friend. So indeed she was, though he had followers, disciples, rivals, competitors, and companions, many degrees of admirers, a biographer, a patron, and a public.

He had also the houseful of sad old women who quarrelled under his beneficent protection. But what friend had he? He was 'solitary' from the day she died.

Let us consider under what solemn conditions and in what immortal phrase the word 'solitary' stands. He wrote it, all Englishmen know where. He wrote it in the hour of that melancholy triumph when he had been at last set free from the dependence upon hope. He hoped no more, and he needed not to hope. The 'notice' of Lord Chesterfield had been too long deferred; it was granted at last, when it was a flattery which Johnson's court of friends would applaud. But not for their sake was it welcome. To no living ear would he bring it and report it with delight.

He was indifferent, he was known. The sensitiveness to pleasure was gone, and the sensitiveness to pain, slights, and neglect would thenceforth be suffered to rest; no man in England would put that to proof again. No man in England, did I say? But, indeed, that is not so. No slight to him, to his person, or to his fame could have had power to cause him pain more sensibly than the customary, habitual, ready-made ridicule that has been cast by posterity upon her whom he loved for twenty years, prayed for during thirty-two years more, who satisfied one of the saddest human hearts, but to whom the world, assiduous to admire him, hardly accords human dignity. He wrote praises of her manners and of her person for her tomb. But her epitaph, that does not name her, is in the greatest of English prose. What was favour to him? 'I am indifferent. . . . I am known. . . . I am solitary, and cannot impart it'.

There has been no denunciation, and perhaps even no recognition, of a certain social immorality in the caricature of the mid-century and earlier. Literary and pictorial alike, it had for its aim the vulgarizing of the married woman. No one now would read Douglas Jerrold for pleasure, but it is worth while to turn up that humourist's serial, 'Mrs. Caudle's Curtain Lectures,' which were presumably considered good comic reading in the 'Punch' of that time, and to make acquaintance with a certain ideal of the grotesque. Obviously to make a serious comment on anything which others consider or have considered humorous is to put oneself at a disadvantage. He who sees the joke holds himself somewhat the superior of the man who would see it, such as it is, if he thought it worth his eyesight. The last-named has to bear the least tolerable of modern reproaches—that he lacks humour; but he need not always care. Now to turn over Douglas Jerrold's monologues is to find that people in the mid-century took their mirth principally from the life of the *arrière boutique*. On that shabby stage was enacted the comedy of literature. Therefore we must take something of the vulgarity of Jerrold as a circumstance of the social ranks wherein he delighted. But the essential vulgarity is that of the woman. There is in some old 'Punch' volume a drawing by Leech—whom one is weary of hearing named the gentle, the refined—where the work of the artist has vied with the spirit of the letterpress. Douglas Jerrold treats of the woman's jealousy, Leech of her stays. They lie on a chair by the bed, beyond description gross. And page by page the woman is derided, with an unfailing enjoyment of her foolish ugliness of person, of manners, and of language. In that time there was, moreover, one great humourist, one whom I infinitely admire; he, too, I am grieved to remember, bore his part willingly in vulgarizing the woman; and the part that fell to him was the vulgarizing of the act of maternity. Woman spiteful, woman suing man at the law for evading her fatuous companionship, woman incoherent, woman abandoned without restraint to violence and temper, woman feigning sensibility—in none of these ignominies is woman so common and so foolish for Dickens as she is in child-bearing.

I named Leech but now. He was, in all things essential, Dickens's contemporary. And accordingly the married woman and her child are humiliated by his pencil; not grossly, but commonly. For him she is moderately and dully ridiculous. What delights him as humorous is that her husband—himself wearisome enough to die of—is weary of her, finds the time long, and tries to escape her. It amuses him that she should furtively spend money over her own dowdiness, to the annoyance of her husband, and that her husband should have no desire to adorn her, and that her mother should be intolerable. It pleases him that her baby, with enormous cheeks and a hideous rosette in its hat—a burlesque baby—should be a grotesque object of her love, for that too makes subtly for her abasement. Charles Keene, again—another contemporary, though he lived into a later and different time. He saw little else than common forms of human ignominy—indignities of civic physique, of stupid prosperity, of dress, of bearing. He transmits these things in greater proportion than he found them—whether for love of the humour of them, or by a kind of inverted disgust that is as eager as delight—one is not sure which is the impulse. The grossness of the vulgarities is rendered with a completeness that goes far to convince us of a certain sensitiveness of apprehension in the designer; and then again we get convinced that real apprehension—real apprehensiveness—would not have insisted upon such things, could not have lived with them through almost a whole career. There is one drawing in the 'Punch' of years ago, in which Charles Keene achieved the nastiest thing possible to even the invention of that day.

A drunken citizen, in the usual broadcloth, has gone to bed, fully dressed, with his boots on and his umbrella open, and the joke lies in the surprise awaiting, when she awakes, the wife asleep at his side in a night-cap. Every one who knows Keene's work can imagine how the huge well-fed figure was drawn, and how the coat wrinkled across the back, and how the bourgeois whiskers were indicated. This obscene drawing is matched by many equally odious. Abject domesticity, ignominies of married life, of middle-age, of money-making; the old common jape against the mother-in-law; abominable weddings: in one drawing a bridegroom with shambling side-long legs asks his bride if she is nervous; she is a widow, and she answers, 'No, never was'. In all these things there is very little humour. Where Keene achieved fun was in the figures of his schoolboys. The hint of tenderness which in really fine work could never be absent from a man's thought of a child or from his touch of one, however frolic or rowdy the subject in hand, is absolutely lacking in Keene's designs; nevertheless, we acknowledge that there is humour. It is also in some of his clerical figures when they are not caricatures, and certainly in 'Robert,' the City waiter of 'Punch'. But so irresistible is the derision of the woman that all Charles Keene's persistent sense of vulgarity is intent centrally upon her. Never for any grace gone astray is she bantered, never for the social extravagances, for prattle, or for beloved dress; but always for her jealousy, and for the repulsive person of the man upon whom she spies and in whom she vindicates her ignoble rights. If this is the shopkeeper the possession of whom is her boast, what then is she?

This great immorality, centring in the irreproachable days of the Exhibition of 1851, or thereabouts—the pleasure in this particular form of human disgrace—has passed, leaving one trace only: the habit by which some men reproach a silly woman through her sex, whereas a silly man is not reproached through his sex. But the vulgarity of which I have written here was distinctively English—the most English thing that England had in days when she bragged of many another—and it was not able to survive an increased commerce of manners and letters with France. It was the chief immorality destroyed by the French novel.

She is eclipsed, or gone, or in hiding. But the sixteenth century took her for granted as the object of song; she was a class, a state, a sex. It was scarcely necessary to waste the lyrist's time—time that went so gaily to metre as not to brook delays—in making her out too clearly. She had no more of what later times call individuality than has the rose, her rival, her foil when she was kinder, her superior when she was cruel, her ever fresh and ever conventional paragon. She needed not to be devised or divined; she was ready. A merry heart goes all the day; the lyrist's never grew weary. Honest men never grow tired of bread or of any other daily things whereof the sweetness is in their own simplicity.

The lady of the lyrics was not loved in mortal earnest, and her punishment now and then for her ingratitude was to be told that she was loved in jest. She did not love; her fancy was fickle; she was not moved by long service, which, by the way, was evidently to be taken for granted precisely like the whole long past of a dream. She had not a good temper. When the poet groans it seems that she has laughed at him; when he flouts her, we may understand that she has chidden her lyrist in no temperate terms. In doing this she has sinned not so much against him as against Love. With that she is perpetually reproved. The lyrist complains to Love, pities Love for her scorning, and threatens to go away with Love, who is on his side. The sweetest verse is tuned to love when the loved one proves worthy.

There is no record of success for this policy. She goes on dancing or scolding, as the case may be, and the lyrist goes on boasting of his constancy, or suddenly renounces it for a day. The situation has variants, but no surprise or ending. The lover's convention is explicit enough, but it might puzzle a reader to account for the lady's. Pride in her beauty, at any rate, is hers—

pride so great that she cannot bring herself to perceive the shortness of her day. She is so unobservant as to need to be told that life is brief, and youth briefer than life; that the rose fades, and so forth.

Now we need not assume that the lady of the lyrics ever lived. But taking her as the perfectly unanimous conception of the lyrists, how is it she did not discover these things unaided? Why does the lover invariably imagine her with a mind intensely irritable under his own praise and poetry? Obviously we cannot have her explanation of any of these matters. Why do the poets so much lament the absence of truth in one whose truth would be of little moment? And why was the convention so pleasant, among all others, as to occupy a whole age—nay, two great ages—of literature?

Music seems to be principally answerable. For the lyrics of the lady are 'words for music' by a great majority. There is hardly a single poem in the Elizabethan Song-books, properly so named, that has what would in our day be called a tone of sentiment. Music had not then the tone herself; she was ingenious, and so must the words be. She had the air of epigram, and an accurately definite limit. So, too, the lady of the lyrics, who might be called the lady of the stanzas, so strictly does she go by measure. When she is quarrelsome, it is but fuguishness; when she dances, she does it by a canon. She could not but be perverse, merrily sung to such grave notes.

So fixed was the law of this perversity that none in the song-books is allowed to be kind enough for a 'melody,' except one lady only. She may thus derogate, for the exceedingly Elizabethan reason that she is 'brown'. She is brown and kind, and a 'sad flower,' but the song made for her would have been too insipid, apparently, without an antithesis. The fair one is warned that her disdain makes her even less lovely than the brown.

Fair as a lily, hard to please, easily angry, ungrateful for innumerable verses, uncertain with the regularity of the madrigal, and inconstant with the punctuality of a stanza, she has gone with the arts of that day; and neither verse nor music will ever make such another lady. She refused to observe the transiency of roses; she never really intended—much as she was urged—to be a shepherdess; she was never persuaded to mitigate her dress. In return, the world has let her disappear. She scorned the poets until they turned upon her in the epigram of many a final couplet; and of these the last has been long written. Her 'No' was set to counterpoint in the part-song, and she frightened Love out of her sight in a ballet. Those occupations are gone, and the lovely Elizabethan has slipped away. She was something less than mortal.

But she who was more than mortal was mortal too. This was no lady of the unanimous lyrists, but a rare visitant unknown to these exquisite little talents. She was not set for singing, but poetry spoke of her; sometimes when she was sleeping, and then Fletcher said—

None can rock Heaven to sleep but her.

Or when she was singing, and Carew rhymed—

Ask me no more whither doth haste
The nightingale when May is past;
For in your sweet dividing throat
She winters, and keeps warm her note.

Sometimes when the lady was dead, and Carew, again, wrote on her monument—

And here the precious dust is laid,
Whose purely-tempered clay was made
So fine that it the guest betrayed.

But there was besides another Lady of the lyrics; one who will never pass from the world, but has passed from song. In the sixteenth century and in the seventeenth century this lady was Death. Her inspiration never failed; not a poet but found it as fresh as the inspiration of life. Fancy was not quenched by the inevitable thought in those days, as it is in ours, and the phrase lost no dignity by the integrity of use.

To every man it happens that at one time of his life—for a space of years or for a space of months—he is convinced of death with an incomparable reality. It might seem as though literature, living the life of a man, underwent that conviction in those ages. Death was as often on the tongues of men in older ages, and oftener in their hands, but in the sixteenth century it was at their hearts. The discovery of death did not shake the poets from their composure. On the contrary, the verse is never measured with more majestic effect than when it moves in honour of this Lady of the lyrics. Sir Walter Raleigh is but a jerky writer when he is rhyming other things, however bitter or however solemn; but his lines on death, which are also lines on immortality, are infinitely noble. These are, needless to say, meditations upon death by law and violence; and so are the ingenious rhymes of Chidiock Tichborne, written after his last prose in his farewell letter to his wife—'Now, Sweet-cheek, what is left to bestow on thee, a small recompense for thy deservings'—and singularly beautiful prose is this. So also are Southwell's words. But these are exceptional deaths, and more dramatic than was needed to awake the poetry of the meditative age.

It was death as the end of the visible world and of the idle business of life—not death as a passage nor death as a fear or a darkness—that was the Lady of the lyrists. Nor was their song of the act of dying. With this a much later and much more trivial literature busied itself. Those two centuries felt with a shock that death would bring an end, and that its equalities would make vain the differences of wit and wealth which they took apparently more seriously than to us seems probable. They never wearied of the wonder. The poetry of our day has an entirely different emotion for death as parting. It was not parting that the lyrists sang of; it was the mere simplicity of death. None of our contemporaries will take such a subject; they have no more than the ordinary conviction of the matter. For the great treatment of obvious things there must evidently be an extraordinary conviction.

But whether the chief Lady of the lyrics be this, or whether she be the implacable Elizabethan feigned by the love-songs, she has equally passed from before the eyes of poets.

Tribulation, Immortality, the Multitude: what remedy of composure do these words bring for their own great disquiet! Without the remoteness of the Latinity the thought would come too close and shake too cruelly. In order to the sane endurance of the intimate trouble of the soul an aloofness of language is needful. Johnson feared death. Did his noble English control and postpone the terror? Did it keep the fear at some courteous, deferent distance from the centre of that human heart, in the very act of the leap and lapse of mortality? Doubtless there is in language such an educative power. Speech is a school. Every language is a persuasion, an induced habit, an instrument which receives the note indeed but gives the tone. Every language imposes a quality, teaches a temper, proposes a way, bestows a tradition: this is the tone—the voice—of the instrument. Every language, by counterchange, returns to the writer's touch or breath his own intention, articulate: this is his note. Much has always been said, many things to the purpose have been thought, of the power and the responsibility of the note. Of the legislation and influence of the tone I have been led to think by comparing the tranquillity of Johnson and the composure of Canning with the stimulated and close emotion, the interior trouble, of those writers who have entered as disciples in the school of the more Teutonic English.

For if every language be a school, more significantly and more educatively is a part of a language a school to him who chooses that part. Few languages offer the choice. The fact that a choice is made implies the results and fruits of a decision. The French author is without these. They are of all the heritages of the English writer the most important. He receives a language of dual derivation. He may submit himself to either University, whither he will take his impulse and his character, where he will leave their influence, and whence he will accept their re-education. The Frenchman has certainly a style to develop within definite limits; but he does not subject himself to suggestions tending mainly hitherwards or thitherwards, to currents of various race within one literature. Such a choice of subjection is the singular opportunity of the Englishman. I do not mean to ignore the necessary mingling. Happily that mingling has been done once for all for us all. Nay, one of the most charming things that a master of English can achieve is the repayment of the united teaching by linking their results so exquisitely in his own practice, that words of the two schools are made to meet each other with a surprise and delight that shall prove them at once gayer strangers, and sweeter companions, than the world knew they were. Nevertheless there remains the liberty of choice as to which school of words shall have the place of honour in the great and sensitive moments of an author's style: which school shall be used for conspicuousness, and which for multitudinous service. And the choice being open, the perturbation of the pulses and impulses of so many hearts quickened in thought and feeling in this day suggests to me a deliberate return to the recollectedness of the more tranquil language. 'Doubtless there is a place of peace'.

A place of peace, not of indifference. It is impossible not to charge some of the moralists of the eighteenth century with an indifference into which they educated their platitudes and into which their platitudes educated them. Addison thus gave and took, until he was almost incapable of coming within arm's-length of a real or spiritual emotion. There is no knowing to what distance the removal of the 'appropriate sentiment' from the central soul might have attained but for the change and renewal in language, which came when it was needed. Addison had assuredly removed eternity far from the apprehension of the soul when his Cato hailed the 'pleasing hope,' the 'fond desire'; and the touch of war was distant from him who conceived his 'repulsed battalions' and his 'doubtful battle'. What came afterwards, when simplicity and nearness were restored once more, was doubtless journeyman's work at times. Men were too eager to go into the workshop of language. There were unreasonable raptures over the mere making of common words. 'A hand-shoe! a finger-hat! a foreword! Beautiful!' they cried; and for the love of German the youngest daughter of Chrysale herself might have consented to be kissed by a grammarian. It seemed to be forgotten that a language with all its construction visible is a language little fitted for the more advanced mental processes; that its images are material; and that, on the other hand, a certain spiritualizing and subtilizing effect of alien derivations is a privilege and an advantage incalculable—that to possess that half of the language within which Latin heredities lurk and Romanesque allusions are at play is to possess the state and security of a dead tongue, without the death.

But now I spoke of words encountering as gay strangers, various in origin, divided in race, within a master's phrase. The most beautiful and the most sudden of such meetings are of course in Shakespeare. 'Superfluous kings,' 'A lass unparalleled,' 'Multitudinous seas': we needed not to wait for the eighteenth century or for the nineteenth or for the twentieth to learn the splendour of such encounters, of such differences, of such nuptial unlikeness and union. But it is well that we should learn them afresh. And it is well, too, that we should not resist the rhythmic reaction bearing us now somewhat to the side of the Latin. Such a reaction is in some sort an ethical need for our day. We want to quell the exaggerated decision of monosyllables. We want the poise and the pause that imply vitality at times better than headstrong movement expresses it. And not the phrase only but the form of verse might render us timely service. The controlling couplet might stay with a touch a modern grief, as it ranged in order the sorrows of Canning for his son. But it should not be attempted without a distinct intention of submission on the part of the writer. The couplet transgressed against, trespassed upon, used loosely, is like a law outstripped, defied—to the dignity neither of the rebel nor of the rule.

To Letters do we look now for the guidance and direction which the very closeness of the emotion taking us by the heart makes necessary. Shall not the Thing more and more, as we compose ourselves to literature, assume the honour, the hesitation, the leisure, the reconciliation of the Word?

REJECTION

Simplicity is not virginal in the modern world. She has a penitential or a vidual singleness. We can conceive an antique world in which life, art, and letters were simple because of the absence of many things; for us now they can be simple only because of our rejection of many things. We are constrained to such a vigilance as will not let even a master's work pass unfanned and unpurged. Even among his phrases one shall be taken and the other left. For he may unawares have allowed the habitualness that besets this multitudinous life to take the pen from his hand and to write for him a page or a word; and habitualness compels our refusals. Or he may have allowed the easy impulse of exaggeration to force a sentence which the mere truth, sensitively and powerfully pausing, would well have become. Exaggeration has played a part of its own in human history. By depreciating our language it has stimulated change, and has kept the circulating word in exercise. Our rejection must be alert and expert to overtake exaggeration and arrest it. It makes us shrewder than we wish to be. And, indeed, the whole endless action of refusal shortens the life we could desire to live. Much of our resolution is used up in the repeated mental gesture of adverse decision. Our tacit and implicit distaste is made explicit, who shall say with what loss to our treasury of quietness? We are defrauded of our interior ignorance, which should be a place of peace. We are forced to confess more articulately than befits our convention with ourselves. We are hurried out of our reluctances. We are made too much aware. Nay, more: we are tempted to the outward activity of destruction; reviewing becomes almost inevitable. As for the spiritual life—O weary, weary act of refusal! O waste but necessary hours, vigil and wakefulness of fear! 'We live by admiration' only a shortened life who live so much in the iteration of rejection and repulse. And in the very touch of joy there hides I know not what ultimate denial; if not on one side, on the other. If joy is given to us without reserve, not so do we give ourselves to joy. We withhold, we close. Having denied many things that have approached us, we deny ourselves to many things. Thus does *il gran rifiuto* divide and rule our world.

Simplicity is worth the sacrifice; but all is not sacrifice. Rejection has its pleasures, the more secret the more unmeasured. When we garnish a house we refuse more furniture, and furniture more various, than might haunt the dreams of decorators. There is no limit to our rejections. And the unconsciousness of the decorators is in itself a cause of pleasure to a mind generous, forbearing, and delicate. When we dress, no fancy may count the things we will none of. When we write, what hinders that we should refrain from Style past reckoning? When we marry——. Moreover, if simplicity is no longer set in a world having the great and beautiful quality of fewness, we can provide an equally fair setting in the quality of refinement. And refinement is not to be achieved but by rejection. One who suggests to me that refinement is apt to be a mere negative has offered up a singular blunder in honour of robustiousness. Refinement is not negative, because it must be compassed by many negations. It is a thing of price as well as of value; it demands immolations, it exacts experience. No slight or easy charge, then, is committed to such of us as, having apprehension of these things, fulfil the office of exclusion. Never before was a time when derogation was always so near, a daily danger, or when the reward of resisting it was so great. The simplicity of literature, more sensitive, more threatened, and more important than other simplicities, needs a guard of honour, who shall never relax the good will nor lose the good heart of their intolerance.

Not without significance is the Spanish nationality of Velasquez. In Spain was the Point put upon Honour; and Velasquez was the first Impressionist. As an Impressionist he claimed, implicitly if not explicitly, a whole series of delicate trusts in his trustworthiness; he made an appeal to the confidence of his peers; he relied on his own candour, and asked that the candid should rely upon him; he kept the chastity of art when other masters were content with its honesty, and when others saved artistic conscience he safeguarded the point of honour. Contemporary masters more or less proved their position, and convinced the world by something of demonstration; the first Impressionist simply asked that his word should be accepted. To those who would not take his word he offers no bond. To those who will, he grants the distinction of a share in his responsibility.

Somewhat unrefined, in comparison with his lofty and simple claim to be believed on a suggestion, is the commoner painter's production of his credentials, his appeal to the sanctions of ordinary experience, his self-defence against the suspicion of making irresponsible mysteries in art. 'You can see for yourself,' the lesser man seems to say to the world, 'thus things are, and I render them in such manner that your intelligence may be satisfied'. This is an appeal to average experience—at the best the cumulative experience; and with the average, or with the sum, art cannot deal without derogation. The Spaniard seems to say: 'Thus things are in my pictorial sight. Trust me, I apprehend them so'. We are not excluded from his counsels, but we are asked to attribute a certain authority to him, master of the craft as he is, master of that art of seeing pictorially which is the beginning and not far from the end—not far short of the whole—of the art of painting. So little indeed are we shut out from the mysteries of a great Impressionist's impression that Velasquez requires us to be in some degree his colleagues. Thus may each of us to whom he appeals take praise from the praised: he leaves my educated eyes to do a little of the work. He respects my responsibility no less—though he respects it less explicitly— than I do his. What he allows me would not be granted by a meaner master. If he does not hold himself bound to prove his own truth, he returns thanks for my trust. It is as though he used his countrymen's courteous hyperbole and called his house my own. In a sense of the most noble hostship he does me the honours of his picture.

Because Impressionism with all its extreme—let us hope its ultimate—derivatives is so free, therefore is it doubly bound. Because there is none to arraign it, it is a thousand times responsible. To undertake this art for the sake of its privileges without confessing its obligations—or at least without confessing them up to the point of honour—is to take a vulgar freedom: to see immunities precisely where there are duties, and an advantage where there is a bond. A very mob of men have taken Impressionism upon themselves, in several forms and under a succession of names, in this our later day. It is against all probabilities that more than a few among these have within them the point of honour. In their galleries we are beset with a dim distrust. And to distrust is more humiliating than to be distrusted. How many of these landscape-painters, deliberately rash, are painting the truth of their own impressions? An ethical question as to loyalty is easily answered; truth and falsehood as to fact are, happily for the intelligence of the common conscience, not hard to divide. But when the *dubium* concerns not fact but artistic truth, can the many be sure that their sensitiveness, their candour, their scruple, their delicate equipoise of perceptions, the vigilance of their apprehension, are enough? Now Impressionists have told us things as to their impressions—as to the effect of things upon the temperament of this man and upon the mood of that—which should not be asserted except on the artistic point of honour. The majority can tell ordinary truth, but should not trust themselves for truth extraordinary. They can face the general judgement, but they should hesitate to produce work that appeals to the last judgement, which is the judgement within. There is too much reason to divine that a certain number of those who aspire to differ from the greatest of masters have no temperaments worth speaking of, no point of view worth seizing, no vigilance worth awaiting, no mood worth waylaying. And to be, *de parti pris*, an Impressionist without these! O Velasquez! Nor is literature quite free from a like reproach in her own things. An author, here and there, will make as though he had a word worth hearing—nay, worth over-hearing—a word that seeks to withdraw even while it is uttered; and yet what it seems to dissemble is all too probably a platitude. But obviously, literature is not—as is the craft and mystery of painting—so at the mercy of a half-imposture, so guarded by unprovable honour. For the art of painting is reserved that shadowy risk, that undefined salvation. If the artistic temperament—tedious word!—with all its grotesque privileges, becomes yet more common than it is, there will be yet less responsibility; for the point of honour is the simple secret of the few.

A serviceable substitute for style in literature has been found in such a collection of language ready for use as may be likened to a portable vocabulary. It is suited to the manners of a day that has produced salad-dressing in bottles, and many other devices for the saving of processes. Fill me such a wallet full of 'graphic' things, of 'quaint' things and 'weird,' of 'crisp' or 'sturdy' Anglo-Saxon, of the material for 'word-painting' (is not that the way of it?), and it will serve the turn. Especially did the Teutonic fury fill full these common little hoards of language. It seemed, doubtless, to the professor of the New Literature that if anything could convince him of his own success it must be the energy of his Teutonisms and his avoidance of languid Latin derivatives, fit only for the pedants of the eighteenth century. Literature doubtless is made of words. What then is needful, he seems to ask, besides a knack of beautiful words? Unluckily for him, he has achieved, not style, but slang. Unluckily for him, words are not style, phrases are not style. 'The man is style'. O good French language, cunning and good, that lets me read the sentence in obverse or converse as I will! And I read it as declaring that the whole man, the very whole of him, is his style. The literature of a man of letters worthy the name is rooted in all his qualities, with little fibres running invisibly into the smallest qualities he has. He who is not a man of letters, simply is not one; it is not too audacious a paradox to affirm that doing will not avail him who fails in being. 'Lay your deadly doing down,' sang once some old hymn known to Calvinists. Certain poets, a certain time ago, ransacked the language for words full of life and beauty, made a vocabulary of them, and out of wantonness wrote them to death. To change somewhat the simile, they scented out a word—an earlyish word, by preference—ran it to earth, unearthed it, dug it out, and killed it. And then their followers bagged it. The very word that lives, 'new every morning,' miraculously new, in the literature of a man of letters, they killed and put into their bag. And, in like manner, the emotion that should have caused the word is dead for those, and for those only, who abuse its expression. For the maker of a portable vocabulary is not content to turn his words up there: he turns up his feelings also, alphabetically or otherwise. Wonderful how much sensibility is at hand in such round words as the New Literature loves. Do you want a generous emotion? Pull forth the little language. Find out moonshine, find out moonshine!

Take, as an instance, Mr. Swinburne's 'hell'. There is, I fear, no doubt whatever that Mr. Swinburne has put his 'hell' into a vocabulary, with the inevitable consequences to the word. And when the minor men of his school have occasion for a 'hell' (which may very well happen to any young man practising authorship), I must not be accused of phantasy if I say that they put their hands into Mr. Swinburne's vocabulary and pick it. These vocabularies are made out of vigorous and blunt language. 'What hempen homespuns have we swaggering here?' Alas, they are homespuns from the factory, machine-made in uncostly quantities. Obviously, power needs to make use of no such storage. The property of power is to use phrases, whether strange or familiar, as though it created them. But even more than lack of power is lack of humour the cause of all the rankness and the staleness, of all the Anglo-Saxon of commerce, of all the weary 'quaintness'—that quaintness of which one is moved to exclaim with Cassio: 'Hither comes the bauble!' Lack of a sense of humour betrays a man into that perpetual too-much whereby he tries to make amends for a currency debased. No more than any other can a witty writer dispense with a sense of humour. In his moments of sentiment the lack is distressing; in his moments of wit it is at least perceptible. A sense of humour cannot be always present, it may be urged. Why, no; it is the lack of it that is—importunate. Other absences, such as the absence of passion, the absence of delicacy, are, if grievous negatives, still mere negatives. These qualities may or may not be there at call, ready for a summons; we are not obliged to know; we are not momentarily aware, unless they ought to be in action, whether their action is possible. But want of power and want of a sense of the ridiculous: these are lacks wherefrom there is no escaping, deficiencies that are all-influential, defects that assert themselves, vacancies that proclaim themselves, absences from the presence whereof there is no flying; what other paradoxes can I adventure? Without power—no style. Without a possible humour,—no style. The weakling has no confidence in himself to keep him from grasping at words that he fancies hold within them the true passions of the race, ready for the uses of his egoism. And with a sense of humour a man will not steal from a shelf the precious treasure of the language and put it in his pocket.

There are hours claimed by Sleep, but refused to him. None the less are they his by some state within the mind, which answers rhythmically and punctually to that claim. Awake and at work, without drowsiness, without languor, and without gloom, the night mind of man is yet not his day mind; he has night-powers of feeling which are at their highest in dreams, but are night's as well as sleep's. The powers of the mind in dreams, which are inexplicable, are not altogether baffled because the mind is awake; it is the hour of their return as it is the hour of a tide's, and they do return.

In sleep they have their free way. Night then has nothing to hamper her influence, and she draws the emotion, the senses, and the nerves of the sleeper. She urges him upon those extremities of anger and love, contempt and terror to which not only can no event of the real day persuade him, but for which, awake, he has perhaps not even the capacity. This increase of capacity, which is the dream's, is punctual to the night, even though sleep and the dream be kept at arm's length.

The child, not asleep, but passing through the hours of sleep and their dominions, knows that the mood of night will have its hour; he postpones his troubled heart, and will answer it another time, in the other state, by day. 'I shall be able to bear this when I am grown up' is not oftener in a young child's mind than 'I shall endure to think of it in the day-time'. By this he confesses the double habit and double experience, not to be interchanged, and communicating together only by memory and hope.

Perhaps it will be found that to work all by day or all by night is to miss something of the powers of a complex mind. One might imagine the rhythmic experience of a poet, subject, like a child, to the time, and tempering the extremities of either state by messages of remembrance and expectancy.

Never to have had a brilliant dream, and never to have had any delirium, would be to live too much in the day; and hardly less would be the loss of him who had not exercised his waking thought under the influence of the hours claimed by dreams. And as to choosing between day and night, or guessing whether the state of day or dark is the truer and the more natural, he would be rash who should make too sure.

In order to live the life of night, a watcher must not wake too much. That is, he should not alter so greatly the character of night as to lose the solitude, the visible darkness, or the quietude. The hours of sleep are too much altered when they are filled by lights and crowds; and Nature is cheated so, and evaded, and her rhythm broken, as when the larks caged in populous streets make ineffectual springs and sing daybreak songs when the London lamps are lighted. Nature is easily deceived; and the muse, like the lark, may be set all astray as to the hour. You may spend the peculiar hours of sleep amid so much noise and among so many people that you shall not be aware of them; you may thus merely force and prolong the day. But to do so is not to live well both lives; it is not to yield to the daily and nightly rise and fall, cradled in the swing of change.

There surely never was a poet but was now and then rocked in such a cradle of alternate hours. 'It cannot be,' says Herbert, 'that I am he on whom Thy tempests fell all night'.

It is in the hours of sleep that the mind, by some divine paradox, has the extremest sense of light. Almost the most shining lines in English poetry—lines that cast sunrise shadows—are those of Blake, written confessedly from the side of night, the side of sorrow and dreams, and those dreams the dreams of little chimney-sweepers; all is as dark as he can make it with the 'bags of soot'; but the boy's dream of the green plain and the river is too bright for day.

So, indeed, is another brightness of Blake's, which is also, in his poem, a child's dream, and was certainly conceived by him in the hours of sleep, in which he woke to write the Songs of Innocence:—

> O what land is the land of dreams?
> What are its mountains, and what are its streams?
> O father, I saw my mother there,
> Among the lilies by waters fair.
> Among the lambs clothèd in white,
> She walk'd with her Thomas in sweet delight.

To none but the hours claimed and inspired by sleep, held awake by sufferance of sleep, belongs such a vision.

Corot also took the brilliant opportunity of the hours of sleep. In some landscapes of his early manner he has the very light of dreams, and it was surely because he went abroad at the time when sleep and dreams claimed his eyes that he was able to see so spiritual an illumination. Summer is precious for a painter, chiefly because in summer so many of the hours of sleep are also hours of light. He carries the mood of man's night out into the sunshine—Corot did so—and lives the life of night, in all its genius, in the presence of a risen sun. In the only time when the heart can dream of light, in the night of visions, with the rhythmic power of night at its dark noon in his mind, his eyes see the soaring of the actual sun.

He himself has not yet passed at that hour into the life of day. To that life belongs many another kind of work, and a sense of other kinds of beauty; but the summer daybreak was seen by Corot with the extreme perception of the life of night. Here, at last, is the explanation of all the memories of dreams recalled by these visionary paintings, done in earlier years than were those, better known, that are the Corots of all the world. Every man who knows what it is to dream of landscape meets with one of these works of Corot's first manner with a cry, not of welcome only, but of recognition. Here is morning perceived by the spirit of the hours of sleep.

The wild man is alone at will, and so is the man for whom civilization has been kind. But there are the multitudes to whom civilization has given little but its reaction, its rebound, its chips, its refuse, its shavings, sawdust and waste, its failures; to them solitude is a right foregone or a luxury unattained; a right foregone, we may name it, in the case of the nearly savage, and a luxury unattained in the case of the nearly refined. These has the movement of the world thronged together into some blind by-way.

Their share in the enormous solitude which is the common, unbounded, and virtually illimitable possession of all mankind has lapsed, unclaimed. They do not know it is theirs. Of many of their kingdoms they are ignorant, but of this most ignorant. They have not guessed that they own for every man a space inviolate, a place of unhidden liberty and of no obscure enfranchisement. They do not claim even the solitude of closed corners, the narrow privacy of the lock and key; nor could they command so much. For the solitude that has a sky and a horizon they know not how to wish.

It lies in a perpetual distance. England has leagues thereof, landscapes, verge beyond verge, a thousand thousand places in the woods, and on uplifted hills. Or rather, solitudes are not to be measured by miles; they are to be numbered by days. They are freshly and freely the dominion of every man for the day of his possession. There is loneliness for innumerable solitaries. As many days as there are in all the ages, so many solitudes are there for men. This is the open house of the earth; no one is refused. Nor is the space shortened or the silence marred because, one by one, men in multitudes have been alone there before. Solitude is separate experience. Nay, solitudes are not to be numbered by days, but by men themselves. Every man of the living and every man of the dead might have had his 'privacy of light'.

It needs no park; it is to be found in the merest working country; and a thicket may be as secret as a forest. It is not so difficult to get for a time out of sight and earshot. Even if your solitude be enclosed, it is still an open solitude, so there be 'no cloister for the eyes,' and a space of far country or a cloud in the sky be privy to your hiding-place. But the best solitude does not hide at all.

This the people who have drifted together into the streets live whole lives and never know. Do they suffer from their deprivation of even the solitude of the hiding-place? There are many who never have a whole hour alone. They live in reluctant or indifferent companionship, as people may in a boarding-house, by paradoxical choice, familiar with one another and not intimate. They live under careless observation and subject to a vagabond curiosity. Theirs is the involuntary and perhaps the unconscious loss which is futile and barren.

One knows the men, and the many women, who have sacrificed all their solitude to the perpetual society of the school, the cloister, or the hospital ward. They walk without secrecy, candid, simple, visible, without moods, unchangeable, in a constant communication and practice of action and speech. Theirs assuredly is no barren or futile loss, and they have a conviction, and they bestow the conviction, of solitude deferred.

Who has painted solitude so that the solitary seemed to stand alone and inaccessible? There is the loneliness of the shepherdess in many a drawing of J. F. Millet. The little figure is away, aloof. The girl stands so when the painter is gone. She waits so on the sun for the closing of the hours of pasture. Millet has her as she looks, out of sight.

Now, although solitude is a prepared, secured, defended, elaborate possession of the rich, they too deny themselves the natural solitude of a woman with a child. A newly-born child is so nursed and talked about, handled and jolted and carried about by aliens, and there is so much importunate service going forward, that a woman is hardly alone long enough to become aware how her own blood in her child moves separately, beside her, with another rhythm and different pulses. All is commonplace until the doors are closed upon the two. This unique intimacy at night is a profound retreat, an absolute seclusion. It is more than single solitude; it is a redoubled isolation more remote than mountains, safer than valleys, deeper than forests, and further than mid-sea.

That solitude partaken—the only partaken solitude in the world—is the Point of Honour of ethics. Treachery to that obligation and a betrayal of that confidence might well be held to be the least pardonable of all crimes. There is no innocent sleep so innocent as sleep shared between a woman and a child, the little breath hurrying beside the longer, as a child's foot runs. But the favourite crime of the sentimentalist is that of a woman against her child. Her power, her intimacy, her opportunity, that should be her accusers, are held to excuse her. She gains the most slovenly of indulgences, on the vulgar plea that her crime was easy. Compassion is due to her on another ground, but not excuse on this.

Lawless and vain art of a certain kind is apt to claim to-day, by the way, some such fondling as a heroine of the dock receives from common opinion. The vain artist had all the advantages. He was master of his own purpose, such as it was; it was his secret, and the public was not privy to his conscience. He does violence to the obligations of which he is aware, and which the world does not know very explicitly. Nothing is easier. Or he is lawless in a more literal sense, but only hopes the world will believe that he has a whole code of his own making. It would, nevertheless, be less unworthy to break obvious rules obviously in the obvious face of the public, and to abide the common rebuke.

It has just been said that a park is by no means necessary for the preparation of a country solitude. Indeed, to make those far and wide and long approaches and avenues to peace seems to be a denial of the accessibility of what should be so simple. A step, a pace or so aside, is enough to lead thither.

A park insists too much, and, besides, does not insist very sincerely. In order to fulfil the apparent professions and to keep the published promise of a park, the owner thereof should be a lover of long seclusion or of a very life of loneliness. He should have gained the state of solitariness which is a condition of life quite unlike any other. The traveller who may have gone astray in countries where an almost life-long solitude is possible knows how invincibly apart are the lonely figures he has seen in desert places there. Their loneliness is broken by his passage, it is true, but hardly so to them. They look at him, but they are not aware that he looks at them. Nay, they look at him as though they were invisible. Their un-self-consciousness is absolute; it is in the wild degree. They are solitaries, body and soul; even when they are curious, and turn to watch the passer-by, they are essentially alone. Now, no one ever found that attitude in a squire's figure, or that look in any country gentleman's eyes. The squire is not a life-long solitary; he never bore himself as though he were invisible. He never had the impersonal ways of a herdsman in the remoter Apennines, with a blind, blank hut in the rocks for his dwelling. Millet would not even have taken him as a model for a solitary in the briefer and milder sylvan solitudes of France. And yet nothing but a life-long, habitual, and wild solitariness would be quite proportionate to a park of any magnitude.

If there is a look of human eyes that tells of perpetual loneliness, so there is also the familiar look that is the sign of perpetual crowds. It is the London expression, and, in its way, the Paris expression. It is the quickly caught, though not interested, look, the dull but ready glance of those who do not know of their forfeited place apart; who have neither the open secret nor the close; no reserve, no need of refuge, no flight nor impulse of flight; no moods but what they may brave out in the street, no hope of news from solitary counsels.

You cannot pass through the real nooks of the world on your own business; they lead nowhere. If you care for them you can rest there awhile; but you must go away back on your own traces. Winds and footsteps drift thither, and find no passage, and the sunshine seems to close there with more remoteness, finality, and peace. A nook is generally of man's work mingled with Nature's, and an old wall generally shuts it off as nobly as any rock. One thing is necessary for a nook—sunshine; without it the place is a mere fag-end of things, and of such London itself is full. Not all on purpose, nor all by chance, was the corner formed; it is disregarded, and its flowers have sown themselves at the wind's will. Colour and light linger late there—

Sunny eve in some forgotten place.

There is a nook at the back of some corner of Hereford Cathedral. No one who has dreamed of places likely to have sun-dials can ever have imagined a more brooding or more forgotten retreat of stone and flowers. Whether there is actually a sun-dial there is of little moment—there are, at any rate, bright grey stones, and they have cracked and parted to give way to the growth of a bygone garden. The place is, of course, a ruin, and a ruin is but indifferently dressed in the green, exact, and lifeless lawns with which the English gardener sometimes invests their overthrow. It is going too far, surely, to weed a ruin and to adorn it with flower-beds in repeating patterns; on the other hand, the mere grass shivers there too coldly without any flowers at all. At least, flowers are necessary for a real nook; and these, at Hereford, are the random flowers that once were set in borders. We inherit the young disorder of the lapse and ruin of a mere border of pansies, as well as the old ruin of the stones. Ours are the venerable times. The mediæval towns were sharp and new, and must have looked, within their walls, like a box of hard toys too tightly packed.

This Hereford corner is beyond and within the cloister; it has no thoroughfare for passing feet; and in the middle is the trace of some old pond or well, which makes little more than a dimple effaced in the careless grass. Nothing more definite remains to suggest the uses of the broken quadrangle. One accustomed to the regulation of monastic buildings suggested the right name of the enclosure of ruin, but I have already forgotten it. In a word, it is as place that many centuries have made, but no other century will see. Either a restorer will come this way, or the ruins will crumble too much and no longer enclose it so exactly, or perhaps a Dean's or a Canon's lawns will approach and embrace the place, and it will become a mere garden. The centuries have given it, by their own slow paradox, a transitory charm.

It is the transitory charm, indeed, so long prepared, that is the almost human beauty of Italy. A little while ago and Venice was not so faded, and a little while hence and she will be more faded, and the sun and salt that have made this tender red by effacement of old colour will efface it more. Italy, needless to say, has many nooks for those who seek them. Great roads along which armies might pass she has, and byways and bridle-paths between her high-walled roads conscious of the outer sunshine, but she has also, in her own perfection, the blind, silent, and neglected enclosure where nothing goes by but time. Such a place, with only one entrance, is the box-hedged forgotten garden by an old villa on the Genoese coast. These box-hedges are very small, hardly a foot high, and they border gravel walks where the pebbles are mixed with Mediterranean shells, and there is more grass than stone or shell. Almond trees, plum-trees, and small cypress trees stand by the high old gate of rusty iron with its hinges set in lichened and broken stone. A prickly pear to the right used to have a mysterious power of tormenting instantly with prickles a child who was so rash as to set foot in its own peculiar path; the air seemed to carry them. The garden is much too old for flowers, except random ones; but the statued fountain in the middle has living water still, and living goldfish. No one else goes thither. There are the broad terraces well in sight, arranged with that majestic sense of approach proper to the Italians of the past—a double flight of stone steps to reach every terrace—one to the right and one to the left, and a cascade fountain with its maidenhair fern in the space enclosed. A great way down, this mountain garden ends in a little landing of a field with a wall—and a view! And a great way down yet again lies the sea round its pines and promontories. All this is a road from the rock to the hill, and you may go your way thereby and come back no more.

Nooks are also by the tideless sea where a rock bars one way, and nooks in the bays where only a boat can enter. But wherever they are, and under whatever sky, they are the figures of certain regions of human thought through which there is no passage. An enclosure not of imprisonment, a finality not of despair are at the end of such thoughts; there is no way beyond, there is no knowledge to reach, there is no explanation, and if a question leads thither there is no solution, and no way out but to retrace your steps in doubt, and but one kind of peace to be had there. The roads of thoughts that are processes, passages, and journeys go by and are open. To the woods there are a thousand gates, and to the freer mountains there are none; to the shifty garden there are two; to the nook there is only one.

Sometimes the eye of a traveller recognizes a nook from a great distance, at a glance, where it lies. A little pasture that seems to soar, higher than an upland valley, is such a nook, and it is a pity to think that one may never see it again; or an English country churchyard that has no wicket; or the melancholy burial-ground of a French village, with its thin black crosses.

There you may count upon solitude, and there are certainly some of the European countries in which solitude, or freedom from the voices of the passing people, is much to be desired— England, unfortunately, the chief of them all. It happened, for example, to the writer to hear a little boy, in the cheerfulness of his heart, attempt to exchange a brief passing conversation on equal terms with two or three passing workmen on a Dover hill. The child had lagged behind his nurse a little, and he took the opportunity of talking to something more masculine, and what he said was but a word of good humour. The workman of fiction would have replied with some hearty phrase having 'young master' in it. What the workman of fact answered to the little boy can be repeated only by dashes, and it ended with 'fool'. 'Gar—you—fool'. An organ grinder would have said, 'Ah, signorino!' It is necessary, in going through such a wayside incident as this, to say to yourself, simply: 'Shakspeare, Crashaw, Milton, Shelley, Wordsworth'. There is no other way, for the time, of enduring the nationality; and whenever the horrible voices one overhears makes the language seem the most intolerable of all languages in sound as well as in significance, it is necessary to say that same charm over, in order to remember well that it is the most heavenly language in the world.

We lose, by mere growing, something of the good habit of familiarity with the old and fresh earth—the familiarity, especially, of the eyes and hands—that is the child's amends for his neglect of the sky. We hold our heads up—or we should do so—and lift our eyes to the horizon and upwards from it, and to the tops of steeples and towers; but the child hardly looks up at all, or no higher than his father's face. It seems that many a grazing and labouring animal feeds through its last long day and draws its last load without having ever looked aloft. Some kinds lift their heads a little when they utter calls or cries, but those are moments of preoccupation, and their attention is not in their eyes.

The eyes of a child, if not so long and so unconsciously bent away as the animals' from the sources of light and darkness and of the rains, are still so little interested in the heights as to need the rising of a bird to show them the way cloudward. The bird leaves a branch shaken, and the hurry of the leaves makes a child look, and, before he is aware that his eyes have taken flight, they are captured by the lark into that unwonted liberty, and beguiled into the manumission of blue sky. The child's sight hardly rises but as an arrow following the bird.

Otherwise the little gaze of those untravelled eyes is busy at close quarters with their own matters. It is not in vain that the senses of children in their simplicity are familiar with delicate shows and scents. While we walk, breathing at the levels of lilac trees and hawthorn, they have to breathe the fresh and strange odour of moss in the woods. Nor is there a breath of the breathing undergrowth that does not find its way to the spirit of a child, to create memories there. Either those wild and most homely scents that are close to the ground have in themselves more significance than have all the richer sweets that blossom breast-high, or else it is their direct communication with childhood that makes them magical. A child without a sense of the earth would miss as much as a child—if one could be—without a sense of the past.

Children poring over the ground make friends of a thousand little creatures that the elders have long ago forgotten. The child knows the spiritual-rustic scent of small daisies, though probably a great number of grown-up people have not been for many consecutive springs at the trouble of smelling a quite small wild daisy; one poet has had so short a memory as to call the daisies 'smell-less'; and so with other kinds of growth. There are ways of the clinging of ivy, many-footed, to be known only on the terms of childhood, and so with the little animals that find their way in the green twilight of blades of grass. Their fortunes are watched by children, who are so near them, and who would—if they might but know something of the work in hand—think themselves happy to use their superior strength and larger outlook in helping the industries of little ants and beetles. This may never be; the errands of the hurry of insects are not to be shared. And even in his consciousness of greater size and all other human conditions, the child is aware of his own one disproportionate disadvantage—he knows well that the ants and beetles are grown up. Only in the business of feeding he finds that he can come to an understanding with all kinds, or nearly all kinds, of small animals, and be useful.

He finds a city of ants most pleasantly responsive; there are no mistakes or misapprehensions. Dear were the ants in a wide stone *loggia* long ago, where they came up through the cracks to take their crumbs in the sunshine, and Benedetta swept them with a besom of destruction, and said in reply to the weeping (and, too probably, the fists) of the children that the ants were not Christians. The little ants—the little grown-up ants, who had something of our respect for aunts, and among whom we perceived differences of size and of manners, were involved in indiscriminate slaughter, like soldiers.

It is at close quarters, near the ground of gardens and fields, that children learn to know the countries, the counties, the north, the south, the orient, and the occident. The country that children pore over is surely the country of memories for which men afterwards die. For this, rather than for any distant plains, or valleys, or even mountains (for which armies have been said to be most willing to take the field). The country that sent the breath and spirit of its earth into the little nostrils of children, that was known in tiny detail, that was known in that low region of the earthy air through which the elders pass with their covered feet—this has always been *patria*.

It is a loss never to have lived young in countries so warm that a child is allowed to feel the grass there with naked feet. For the feet also ought to have communication with the fields; they have their own sensation of flowers. Even as all the senses are distinct and different, and as it were a separate conception of the mind, so also are the sensibilities. They are not merely added ways of communion, they are all unique ways. To lack the sensibility of feet that might have been acquainted with various Nature, but that had their tenderness touched by nothing save dead sand at the seaside, is a little loss that one wishes the civilized child had not to undergo.

A poppy bud, packed into tight bundles by so hard and resolute a hand that the petals of the flower never afterwards lose the creases, is a type of the child. Nothing but the unfolding, which is as yet in the non-existing future, can explain the manner of the close folding of character. In both flower and child it looks much as though the process had been the reverse of what it was—as though a finished and open thing had been folded up into the bud—so plainly and certainly is the future implied, and the intention of compressing and folding-close made manifest.

With the other incidents of childish character, the crowd of impulses called 'naughtiness' is perfectly perceptible—it would seem heartless to say how soon. The naughty child (who is often an angel of tenderness and charm, affectionate beyond the capacity of his fellows, and a very ascetic of penitence when the time comes) opens early his brief campaigns and raises the standard of revolt as soon as he is capable of the desperate joys of disobedience.

But even the naughty child is an individual, and must not be treated in the mass. He is numerous indeed, but not general, and to describe him you must take the unit, with all his incidents and his organic qualities as they are. Take then, for instance, one naughty child in the reality of his life. He is but six years old, slender and masculine, and not wronged by long hair, curls, or effeminate dress. His face is delicate and too often haggard with tears of penitence that Justice herself would be glad to spare him. Some beauty he has, and his mouth especially is so lovely as to seem not only angelic but itself an angel. He has absolutely no self-control and his passions find him without defence. They come upon him in the midst of his usual brilliant gaiety and cut short the frolic comedy of his fine spirits.

Then for a wild hour he is the enemy of the laws. If you imprison him, you may hear his resounding voice as he takes a running kick at the door, shouting his justification in unconquerable rage. 'I'm good now!' is made as emphatic as a shot by the blow of his heel upon the panel. But if the moment of forgiveness is deferred, in the hope of a more promising repentance, it is only too likely that he will betake himself to a hostile silence and use all the revenge yet known to his imagination. 'Darling mother, open the door!' cries his touching voice at last; but if the answer should be 'I must leave you for a short time, for punishment,' the storm suddenly thunders again. 'There (crash!) I have broken a plate, and I'm glad it is broken into such little pieces that you can't mend it. I'm going to break the 'lectric light'. When things are at this pass there is one way, and only one, to bring the child to an overwhelming change of mind; but it is a way that would be cruel, used more than twice or thrice in his whole career of tempest and defiance. This is to let him see that his mother is troubled. 'Oh, don't cry! Oh, don't be sad!' he roars, unable still to deal with his own passionate anger, which is still dealing with him. With his kicks of rage he suddenly mingles a dance of apprehension lest his mother should have tears in her eyes. Even while he is still explicitly impenitent and defiant he tries to pull her round to the light that he may see her face. It is but a moment before the other passion of remorse comes to make havoc of the helpless child, and the first passion of anger is quelled outright.

Only to a trivial eye is there nothing tragic in the sight of these great passions within the small frame, the small will, and, in a word, the small nature. When a large and sombre fate befalls a little nature, and the stage is too narrow for the action of a tragedy, the disproportion has sometimes made a mute and unexpressed history of actual life or sometimes a famous book; it is the manifest core of George Eliot's story of 'Adam Bede,' where the suffering of Hetty is, as it were, the eye of the storm. All is expressive around her, but she is hardly articulate; the book is full of words—preachings, speeches, daily talk, aphorisms, but a space of silence remains about her in the midst of the story. And the disproportion of passion—the inner disproportion—is at least as tragic as that disproportion of fate and action; it is less intelligible, and leads into the intricacies of nature which are more difficult than the turn of events.

It seems, then, that this passionate play is acted within the narrow limits of a child's nature far oftener than in a nature adult and finally formed. And this, evidently, because there is unequal force at work within a child, unequal growth and a jostling of powers and energies that are hurrying to their development and pressing for exercise and life. It is this helpless inequality—this untimeliness—that makes the guileless comedy mingling with the tragedies of a poor child's day. He knows thus much—that life is troubled around him and that the fates are strong. He implicitly confesses 'the strong hours' of antique song. This same boy—the tempestuous child of passion and revolt—went out with quiet cheerfulness for a walk lately, saying as his cap was put on, 'Now, mother, you are going to have a little peace'. This way of accepting his own conditions is shared by a sister, a very little older, who, being of an equal and gentle temper, indisposed to violence of every kind and tender to all without disquiet, observes the boy's brief frenzies as a citizen observes the climate. She knows the signs quite well and can at any time give the explanation of some particular outburst, but without any attempt to go in search of further or more original causes. Still less is she moved by the virtuous indignation that is the least charming of the ways of some little girls. *Elle ne fait que constater.* Her equanimity has never been overset by the wildest of his moments, and she has witnessed them all. It is needless to say that she is not frightened by his drama, for Nature takes care that her young creatures shall not be injured by sympathies. Nature encloses them in the innocent indifference that preserves their brains from the more harassing kinds of distress.

Even the very frenzy of rage does not long dim or depress the boy. It is his repentance that makes him pale, and Nature here has been rather forced, perhaps—with no very good result. Often must a mother wish that she might for a few years govern her child (as far as he is governable) by the lowest motives—trivial punishments and paltry rewards—rather than by any kind of appeal to his sensibilities. She would wish to keep the words 'right' and 'wrong' away from his childish ears, but in this she is not seconded by her lieutenants. The child himself is quite willing to close with her plans, in so far as he is able, and is reasonably interested in the results of her experiments. He wishes her attempts in his regard to have a fair chance. 'Let's hope I'll be good all to-morrow,' he says with the peculiar cheerfulness of his ordinary voice. 'I do hope so, old man'. 'Then I'll get my penny. Mother, I was only naughty once yesterday; if I have only one naughtiness to-morrow, will you give me a halfpenny?' 'No reward except for real goodness all day long'. 'All right'.

It is only too probable that this system (adopted only after the failure of other ways of reform) will be greatly disapproved as one of bribery. It may, however, be curiously inquired whether all kinds of reward might not equally be burlesqued by that word, and whether any government, spiritual or civil, has ever even professed to deny rewards. Moreover, those who would not give a child a penny for being good will not hesitate to fine him a penny for being naughty, and rewards and punishments must stand or fall together. The more logical objection will be that goodness is ideally the normal condition, and that it should have, therefore, no explicit extraordinary result, whereas naughtiness, being abnormal, should have a visible and unusual sequel. To this the rewarding mother may reply that it is not reasonable to take 'goodness' in a little child of strong passions as the normal condition. The natural thing for him is to give full sway to impulses that are so violent as to overbear his powers.

But, after all, the controversy returns to the point of practice. What is the thought, or threat, or promise that will stimulate the weak will of the child, in the moment of rage and anger, to make a sufficient resistance? If the will were naturally as well developed as the passions, the stand would be soon made and soon successful; but as it is there must needs be a bracing by the suggestion of joy or fear. Let, then, the stimulus be of a mild and strong kind at once, and mingled with the thought of distant pleasure. To meet the suffering of rage and frenzy by the suffering of fear is assuredly to make of the little unquiet mind a battle-place of feelings too hurtfully tragic. The penny is mild and strong at once, with its still distant but certain joys of purchase; the promise and hope break the mood of misery, and the will takes heart to resist and conquer.

It is only in the lesser naughtiness that he is master of himself. The lesser the evil fit the more deliberate. So that his mother, knowing herself to be not greatly feared, once tried to mimic the father's voice with a menacing, 'What's that noise?' The child was persistently crying and roaring on an upper floor, in contumacy against his French nurse, when the barytone and threatening question was sent pealing up the stairs. The child was heard to pause and listen and then to say to his nurse, '*Ce n'est pas Monsieur; c'est Madame,*' and then, without further loss of time, to resume the interrupted clamours.

Obviously, with a little creature of six years, there are two things mainly to be done—to keep the delicate brain from the evil of the present excitement, especially the excitement of painful feeling, and to break the habit of passion. Now that we know how certainly the special cells of the brain which are locally affected by pain and anger become hypertrophied by so much use, and all too ready for use in the future at the slightest stimulus, we can no longer slight the importance of habit. Any means, then, that can succeed in separating a little child from the habit of anger does fruitful work for him in the helpless time of his childhood. The work is not easy, but a little thought should make it easy for the elders to avoid the provocation which they—who should ward off provocations—are apt to bring about by sheer carelessness. It is only in childhood that our race knows such physical abandonment to sorrow and tears, as a child's despair; and the theatre with us must needs copy childhood if it would catch the note and action of a creature without hope.

There is a certain year that is winged, as it were, against the flight of time; it does so move, and yet withstands time's movement. It is full of pauses that are due to the energy of change, has bounds and rebounds, and when it is most active then it is longest. It is not long with languor. It has room for remoteness, and leisure for oblivion. It takes great excursions against time, and travels so as to enlarge its hours. This certain year is any one of the early years of fully conscious life, and therefore it is of all the dates. The child of Tumult has been living amply and changefully through such a year—his eighth. It is difficult to believe that his is a year of the self-same date as that of the adult, the men who do not breast their days.

For them is the inelastic, or but slightly elastic, movement of things. Month matched with month shows a fairly equal length. Men and women never travel far from yesterday; nor is their morrow in a distant light. There is recognition and familiarity between their seasons. But the Child of Tumult has infinite prospects in his year. Forgetfulness and surprise set his east and his west at immeasurable distance. His Lethe runs in the cheerful sun. You look on your own little adult year, and in imagination enlarge it, because you know it to be the contemporary of his. Even she who is quite old, if she have a vital fancy, may face a strange and great extent of a few years of her life still to come—his years, the years she is to live at his side.

Reason seems to be making good her rule in this little boy's life, not so much by slow degrees as by sudden and fitful accessions. His speech is yet so childish that he chooses, for a toy, with blushes of pleasure, 'a little duck what can walk'; but with a beautifully clear accent he greets his mother with the colloquial question, 'Well, darling, do you know the latest?' 'The *what?*' 'The latest: do you know the latest?' And then he tells his news, generally, it must be owned, with some reference to his own wrongs. On another occasion the unexpected little phrase was varied; the news of the war then raging distressed him; a thousand of the side he favoured had fallen. The child then came to his mother's room with the question: 'Have you heard the saddest?' Moreover the 'saddest' caused him several fits of perfectly silent tears, which seized him during the day, on his walks or at other moments of recollection. From such great causes arise such little things! Some of his grief was for the nation he admired, and some was for the triumph of his brother, whose sympathies were on the other side, and who perhaps did not spare his sensibilities.

The tumults of a little child's passions of anger and grief, growing fewer as he grows older, rather increase than lessen in their painfulness. There is a fuller consciousness of complete capitulation of all the childish powers to the overwhelming compulsion of anger. This is not temptation; the word is too weak for the assault of a child's passion upon his will. That little will is taken captive entirely, and before the child was seven he knew that it was so. Such a consciousness leaves all babyhood behind and condemns the child to suffer. For a certain passage of his life he is neither unconscious of evil, as he was, nor strong enough to resist it, as he will be. The time of the subsiding of the tumult is by no means the least pitiable of the phases of human life. Happily the recovery from each trouble is ready and sure; so that the child who had been abandoned to naughtiness with all his will in an entire consent to the gloomy possession of his anger, and who had later undergone a haggard repentance, has his captivity suddenly turned again, 'like rivers in the south'. 'Forget it,' he had wept, in a kind of extremity of remorse; 'forget it, darling, and don't, don't be sad'; and it is he, happily, who forgets. The wasted look of his pale face is effaced by the touch of a single cheerful thought, and five short minutes can restore the ruin, as though a broken little German town should in the twinkling of an eye be restored as no architect could restore it—should be made fresh, strong, and tight again, looking like a full box of toys, as a town was wont to look in the new days of old.

When his ruthless angers are not in possession the child shows the growth of this tardy reason that—quickened—is hereafter to do so much for his peace and dignity, by the sweetest consideration. Denied a second handful of strawberries, and seeing quite clearly that the denial was enforced reluctantly, he makes haste to reply, 'It doesn't matter, darling'. At any sudden noise in the house his beautiful voice, with all its little difficulties of pronunciation, is heard with the sedulous reassurance: 'It's all right, mother, nobody hurted ourselves!' He is not surprised so as to forget this gentle little duty, which was never required of him, but is of his own devising.

According to the opinion of his dear and admired American friend, he says all these things, good and evil, with an English accent; and at the American play his English accent was irrepressible. 'It's too comic; no, it's too comic,' he called in his enjoyment; being the only perfectly fearless child in the world, he will not consent to the conventional shyness in public, whether he be the member of an audience or of a congregation, but makes himself perceptible. And even when he has a desperate thing to say, in the moment of absolute revolt—such a thing as 'I *can't* like you, mother,' which anon he will recant with convulsions of distress—he has to 'speak the thing he will,' and when he recants it is not for fear.

If such a child could be ruled (or approximately ruled, for inquisitorial government could hardly be so much as attempted) by some small means adapted to his size and to his physical aspect, it would be well for his health, but that seems at times impossible. By no effort can his elders altogether succeed in keeping tragedy out of the life that is so unready for it. Against great emotions no one can defend him by any forethought. He is their subject; and to see him thus devoted and thus wrung, thus wrecked by tempests inwardly, so that you feel grief has him actually by the heart, recalls the reluctance—the question—wherewith you perceive the interior grief of poetry or of a devout life. Cannot the Muse, cannot the Saint, you ask, live with something less than this? If this is the truer life, it seems hardly supportable. In like manner it should be possible for a child of seven to come through his childhood with griefs that should not so closely involve him, but should deal with the easier sentiments.

Despite all his simplicity, the child has (by way of inheritance, for he has never heard them) the self-excusing fictions of our race. Accused of certain acts of violence, and unable to rebut the charge with any effect, he flies to the old convention: 'I didn't know what I was doing,' he avers, using a great deal of gesticulation to express the temporary distraction of his mind. 'Darling, after nurse slapped me as hard as she could, I didn't know what I was doing, so I suppose I pushed her with my foot'. His mother knows as well as does Tolstoi that men and children know what they are doing, and are the more intently aware as the stress of feeling makes the moments more tense; and she will not admit a plea which her child might have learned from the undramatic authors he has never read.

Far from repenting of her old system of rewards, and far from taking fright at the name of a bribe, the mother of the Child of Tumult has only to wish she had at command rewards ample and varied enough to give the shock of hope and promise to the heart of the little boy, and change his passion at its height.

To mount a hill is to lift with you something lighter and brighter than yourself or than any meaner burden. You lift the world, you raise the horizon; you give a signal for the distance to stand up. It is like the scene in the Vatican when a Cardinal, with his dramatic Italian hands, bids the kneeling groups to arise. He does more than bid them. He lifts them, he gathers them up, far and near, with the upward gesture of both arms; he takes them to their feet with the compulsion of his expressive force. Or it is as when a conductor takes his players to successive heights of music. You summon the sea, you bring the mountains, the distances unfold unlooked-for wings and take an even flight. You are but a man lifting his weight upon the upward road, but as you climb the circle of the world goes up to face you.

Not here or there, but with a definite continuity, the unseen unfolds. This distant hill outsoars that less distant, but all are on the wing, and the plain raises its verge. All things follow and wait upon your eyes. You lift these up, not by the raising of your eyelids, but by the pilgrimage of your body. 'Lift thine eyes to the mountains'. It is then that other mountains lift themselves to your human eyes.

It is the law whereby the eye and the horizon answer one another that makes the way up a hill so full of universal movement. All the landscape is on pilgrimage. The town gathers itself closer, and its inner harbours literally come to light; the headlands repeat themselves; little cups within the treeless hills open and show their farms. In the sea are many regions. A breeze is at play for a mile or two, and the surface is turned. There are roads and curves in the blue and in the white. Not a step of your journey up the height that has not its replies in the steady motion of land and sea. Things rise together like a flock of many-feathered birds.

But it is the horizon, more than all else, you have come in search of; that is your chief companion on your way. It is to uplift the horizon to the equality of your sight that you go high. You give it a distance worthy of the skies. There is no distance, except the distance in the sky, to be seen from the level earth; but from the height is to be seen the distance of this world. The line is sent back into the remoteness of light, the verge is removed beyond verge, into a distance that is enormous and minute.

So delicate and so slender is the distant horizon that nothing less near than Queen Mab and her chariot can equal its fineness. Here on the edges of the eyelids, or there on the edges of the world—we know no other place for things so exquisitely made, so thin, so small and tender. The touches of her passing, as close as dreams, or the utmost vanishing of the forest or the ocean in the white light between the earth and the air; nothing else is quite so intimate and fine. The extremities of a mountain view have just such tiny touches as the closeness of closed eyes shuts in.

On the horizon is the sweetest light. Elsewhere colour mars the simplicity of light; but there colour is effaced, not as men efface it, by a blur or darkness, but by mere light. The bluest sky disappears on that shining edge; there is not substance enough for colour. The rim of the hill, of the woodland, of the meadow-land, of the sea—let it only be far enough—has the same absorption of colour; and even the dark things drawn upon the bright edges of the sky are lucid, the light is among them, and they are mingled with it. The horizon has its own way of making bright the pencilled figures of forests, which are black but luminous.

On the horizon, moreover, closes the long perspective of the sky. There you perceive that an ordinary sky of clouds— not a thunder sky—is not a wall but the underside of a floor. You see the clouds that repeat each other grow smaller by distance; and you find a new unity in the sky and earth that gather alike the great lines of their designs to the same distant close. There is no longer an alien sky, tossed up in unintelligible heights.

Of all the things that London has foregone, the most to be regretted is the horizon. Not the bark of the trees in its right colour; not the spirit of the growing grass, which has in some way escaped from the parks; not the smell of the earth unmingled with the odour of soot; but rather the mere horizon. No doubt the sun makes a beautiful thing of the London smoke at times, and in some places of the sky; but not there, not where the soft sharp distance ought to shine. To be dull there is to put all relations and comparisons in the wrong, and to make the sky lawless.

A horizon dark with storm is another thing. The weather darkens the line and defines it, or mingles it with the raining cloud; or softly dims it, or blackens it against a gleam of narrow sunshine in the sky. The stormy horizon will take wing, and the sunny. Go high enough, and you can raise the light from beyond the shower, and the shadow from behind the ray. Only the shapeless and lifeless smoke disobeys and defeats the summons of the eyes.

Up at the top of the seaward hill your first thought is one of some compassion for sailors, inasmuch as they see but little of their sea. A child on a mere Channel cliff looks upon spaces and sizes that they cannot see in the Pacific, on the ocean side of the world. Never in the solitude of the blue water, never between the Cape of Good Hope and Cape Horn, never between the Islands and the West, has the seaman seen anything but a little circle of sea. The Ancient Mariner, when he was alone, did but drift through a thousand narrow solitudes. The sailor has nothing but his mast, indeed. And but for his mast he would be isolated in as small a world as that of a traveller through the plains.

A close circlet of waves is the sailor's famous offing. His offing hardly deserves the name of horizon. To hear him you might think something of his offing, but you do not so when you sit down in the centre of it.

As the upspringing of all things at your going up the heights, so steady, so swift, is the subsidence at your descent. The further sea lies away, hill folds down behind hill. The whole upstanding world, with its looks serene and alert, its distant replies, its signals of many miles, its signs and communications of light, gathers down and pauses. This flock of birds which is the mobile landscape wheels and goes to earth. The Cardinal weighs down the audience with his downward hands. Farewell to the most delicate horizon.

CLOUD

During a part of the year London does not see the clouds. Not
to see the clear sky might seem her chief loss, but that is shared
by the rest of England, and is, besides, but a slight privation.
Not to see the clear sky is, elsewhere, to see the cloud. But not
so in London. You may go for a week or two at a time, even
though you hold your head up as you walk, and even though
you have windows that really open, and yet you shall see no
cloud, or but a single edge, the fragment of a form.

Guillotine windows never wholly open, but are filled with
a doubled glass towards the sky when you open them towards
the street. They are, therefore, a sure sign that for all the years
when no other windows were used in London, nobody there
cared much for the sky, or even knew so much as whether
there were a sky.

But the privation of cloud is indeed a graver loss than
the world knows. Terrestrial scenery is much, but it is not all.
Men go in search of it; but the celestial scenery journeys to
them; it goes its way round the world. It has no nation, it costs
no weariness, it knows no bonds. The terrestrial scenery—
the tourist's—is a prisoner compared with this. The tourist's
scenery moves indeed, but only like Wordsworth's maiden,
with earth's diurnal course; it is made as fast as its own graves.
And for its changes it depends upon the mobility of the skies.
The mere green flushing of its own sap makes only the least
of its varieties; for the greater it must wait upon the visits of
the light. Spring and autumn are inconsiderable events in a
landscape compared with the shadows of a cloud.

The cloud controls the light, and the mountains on earth
appear or fade according to its passage; they wear so simply,
from head to foot, the luminous grey or the emphatic purple,
as the cloud permits, that their own local colour and their own

local season are lost and cease, effaced before the all-important mood of the cloud.

The sea has no mood except that of the sky and of its winds. It is the cloud that, holding the sun's rays in a sheaf as a giant holds a handful of spears, strikes the horizon, touches the extreme edge with a delicate revelation of light, or suddenly puts it out and makes the foreground shine.

Every one knows the manifest work of the cloud when it descends and partakes in the landscape obviously, lies half-way across the mountain slope, stoops to rain heavily upon the lake, and blots out part of the view by the rough method of standing in front of it. But its greatest things are done from its own place, aloft. Thence does it distribute the sun.

Thence does it lock away between the hills and valleys more mysteries than a poet conceals, but, like him, not by interception. Thence it writes out and cancels all the tracery of Monte Rosa, or lets the pencils of the sun renew them. Thence, hiding nothing, and yet making dark, it sheds deep colour upon the forest land of Sussex, so that, seen from the hills, all the country is divided between grave blue and graver sunlight.

And all this is but its influence, its secondary work upon the world. Its own beauty is unaltered when it has no earthly beauty to improve. It is always great: above the street, above the suburbs, above the gas-works and the stucco, above the faces of painted white houses—the painted surfaces that have been devised as the only things able to vulgarise light, as they catch it and reflect it grotesquely from their importunate gloss. This is to be well seen on a sunny evening in Regent Street.

Even here the cloud is not so victorious as when it towers above some little landscape of rather paltry interest—a conventional river heavy with water, gardens with their little evergreens, walks, and shrubberies; and thick trees impervious to the light, touched, as the novelists always have it, with 'autumn tints'. High over these rises, in the enormous scale of the scenery of clouds, what no man expected—an heroic sky. Few of the things that were ever done upon earth are great enough to be done under such a heaven. It was surely designed for other days. It is for an epic world. Your eyes sweep a thousand miles of cloud. What are the distances of earth to these, and what are the distances of the clear and cloudless sky? The very horizons of the landscape are near, for the round world dips so soon; and the distances of the mere clear sky are unmeasured—you rest upon nothing until you come to a star, and the star itself is immeasurable.

But in the sky of 'sunny Alps' of clouds the sight goes farther, with conscious flight, than it could ever have journeyed otherwise. Man would not have known distance veritably without the clouds. There are mountains indeed, precipices and deeps, to which those of the earth are pigmy. Yet the sky-heights, being so far off, are not overpowering by disproportion, like some futile building fatuously made too big for the human measure. The cloud in its majestic place composes with a little Perugino tree. For you stand or stray in the futile building, while the cloud is no mansion for man, and out of reach of his limitations.

The cloud, moreover, controls the sun, not merely by keeping the custody of his rays, but by becoming the counsellor of his temper. The cloud veils an angry sun, or, more terribly, lets fly an angry ray, suddenly bright upon tree and tower, with iron-grey storm for a background. Or when anger had but threatened, the cloud reveals him, gentle beyond hope. It makes peace, constantly, just before sunset.

It is in the confidence of the winds, and wears their colours. There is a heavenly game, on south-west wind days, when the clouds are bowled by a breeze from behind the evening. They are round and brilliant, and come leaping up from the horizon for hours. This is a frolic and haphazard sky.

All unlike this is the sky that has a centre, and stands composed about it. As the clouds marshalled the earthly mountains, so the clouds in turn are now ranged. The tops of all the celestial Andes aloft are swept at once by a single ray, warmed with a single colour. Promontory after league-long promontory of a stiller Mediterranean in the sky is called out of mist and grey by the same finger. The cloudland is very great, but a sunbeam makes all its nations and continents sudden with light.

All this is for the untravelled. All the winds bring him this scenery. It is only in London, for part of the autumn and part of the winter, that the unnatural smoke-fog comes between. And for many and many a day no London eye can see the horizon, or the first threat of the cloud like a man's hand. There never was a great painter who had not exquisite horizons, and if Corot and Crome were right, the Londoner loses a great thing.

He loses the coming of the cloud, and when it is high in air he loses its shape. A cloud-lover is not content to see a snowy and rosy head piling into the top of the heavens; he wants to see the base and the altitude. The perspective of a cloud is a great part of its design—whether it lies so that you can look along the immense horizontal distances of its floor, or whether it rears so upright a pillar that you look up its mountain steeps in the sky as you look at the rising heights of a mountain that stands, with you, on the earth.

The cloud has a name suggesting darkness; nevertheless, it is not merely the guardian of the sun's rays and their director. It is the sun's treasurer; it holds the light that the world has lost. We talk of sunshine and moonshine, but not of cloud-shine, which is yet one of the illuminations of our skies. A shining cloud is one of the most majestic of all secondary lights. If the reflecting moon is the bride, this is the friend of the bridegroom.

Needless to say, the cloud of a thunderous summer is the most beautiful of all. It has spaces of a grey for which there is no name, and no other cloud looks over at a vanishing sun from such heights of blue air. The shower-cloud, too, with its thin edges, comes across the sky with so influential a flight that no ship going out to sea can be better worth watching. The dullest thing perhaps in the London streets is that people take their rain there without knowing anything of the cloud that drops it. It is merely rain, and means wetness. The shower-cloud there has limits of time, but no limits of form, and no history whatever. It has not come from the clear edge of the plain to the south, and will not shoulder anon the hill to the north. The rain, for this city, hardly comes or goes; it does but begin and stop. No one looks after it on the path of its retreat.

Another good reason for leaving blank, unvexed, and unencumbered with paper patterns the ceiling and walls of a simple house is that the plain surface may be visited by the unique designs of shadows. The opportunity is so fine a thing that it ought oftener to be offered to the light and to yonder handful of long sedges and rushes in a vase. Their slender grey design of shadows upon your white walls is better than a tedious, trivial, or anxious repetition of diaper or flowers in colours.

The shadow has all intricacies of perspective simply translated into line and intersecting curve, and pictorially presented to the eyes, not to the mind. The shadow knows nothing except its flat designs. It is single; it draws a decoration that was never seen before, and will never be seen again, and that, untouched, varies with the journey of the sun, shifts the inter-relation of a score of delicate lines at the mere passing of time, though all the room be motionless. There is, after all, a dreadful fixity in all other drawings. Why will art insist upon its importunate immortality? Wiser is the drama, and wiser the dance, that do not pause upon an attitude. But these walk with passion or pleasure, while the shadow walks with the earth. It alters as the hours wheel. Moreover, while the habit of your sunward thoughts is still flowing southward, after the winter and the spring, it surprises you in the sudden gleam of a north-westering sun. It decks a new wall; it is shed by a late sunset through a window unvisited for a year past; it betrays the flitting of the sun into unwonted skies—a sun that takes the midsummer world in the rear, and is about to alight on an unused horizon. So does the grey drawing, with which you have allowed the sun and your pot of rushes to adorn your room, play the stealthy game of the year.

But the luxury, the extravagance of shadows, is for lamplight. With the tender designs of lamplight shadows you can make your plain room ready for a gala night. It is a festival of leaves and lines, and you can let your fancy go wild, as the London house-holder's does in the ordering of upholsteries of a more solid kind and paintings out of the exhibitions. You need not stint yourself of shadows, for an occasion. These, too, the lamps cast upon your ceiling, which the sun shadows leave unvisited. And it is the best field for this manner of decoration, inasmuch as, however plain your surfaces may be, the ceiling is generally still the plainest. These two lamps make of one palm-branch a symmetrical countercharge of shadows, and here two palm-branches close with one another in shadow, their arches flowing together, and their paler greys darkening. It is hard to believe that there is an enormous majority of people who prefer a 'repeating pattern'.

In fact, it is difficult to persuade a world so persistently busy in the work of spoiling the simplicity of surfaces that shadows are in any sense a sufficient decoration. Nay, it does not see them. It will speak of a blank wall, and apparently will see it as a blank, even when the warm white is but the ground of a wavering, various, and sensitive 'impression' of shades. We are often told that the artist should learn to leave out; but it would seem that it is the absolutely unpictorial man who habitually leaves out, who is unaware of things that would be conspicuous to a simple eye, and who has a trick of seeing local colour, for instance, without its thousand accidents of air, of climate, and of light. Nevertheless, one must grant to him that a grey day robs of their decoration the walls that should be sprinkled with day-shadows. But why should not a plaque or a picture be kept for hanging on shadowless days? To dress a room once for all, and to give it no more heed, is to neglect the units of the days.

But indoor shadows are only messages from that world of shadows which is the landscape of mid-May. Facing a May sun you see little except an infinite number of shadows. Atoms of shadow—be the day bright enough—compose the very air through which you see the light. The trees show you a shadow for every leaf, and the poplars are sprinkled upon the shining sky with little shadows that look translucent. The liveliness of every shadow is that some light is reflected into it; shade and shine have been entangled as though by some wild wind through their million molecules. Only if you turn your back on the sun are all the innumerable shadows eclipsed and effaced. Turn southward again and they come to life, and are themselves the life, the activity, and the transparence of the day.

To eyes tired and retired all day within lowered blinds, the light looks still and changeless. So many squares of sunshine abide for so many hours, and when the sun has circled away they pass and are extinguished. Him who lies alone there is less touched by the long sunshine than by the haste and passage of a shadow. That sign of the sun visits him more brilliantly than does the sunlight. Although there may be no tree to stand between his window and the south, and although no noonday wind may blow a branch of roses across the blind, shadows and their life will be carried across by a bird. To the sick man a cloud-shadow is nothing but an eclipse; he cannot see its shape, its colour, its approach, or its flight. It does but darken his window as it darkens the day, and is gone again; he does not see it pluck and snatch the sunshine, and for him it has no edge. But the flying bird shows him wings. What flash of light could be more bright for him than such a flash of darkness? It is the pulse of life, where all change had seemed to be charmed. If he had seen the bird itself he would have seen less—the bird's shadow was a message from the sun. There are two separated flights for the fancy to follow, the flight of the bird in the air, and the flight of its shadow on earth. This goes across the window blind, across the wood, where it is astray for a while in the shades; it dips into the valley, growing vaguer and larger, runs, quicker than the wind, uphill, smaller and darker on the soft and dry grass, and rushes to meet its bird when the bird swoops to a branch and clings.

In the great bird country of the north-eastern littoral of England, about Holy Island and the basaltic rocks, the shadows of the high birds are the movement and the beating heart of the solitude. Where there are no woods to dip and ripple and make a shade, the sun suffers the brilliant eclipse of flocks of pearl-white sea birds, or of the solitary creature driving on the wind. Theirs is always a surprise of flight. The clouds go one way, but the birds go all ways: in from the sea or out, across the sands, inland to high northern fields, where the crops are late by a month. They fly so high that though they have the shadow of the sun under their wings, they have the light of the earth there also. The waves and the coast shine up to them, and they fly between lights. Black flocks and white they gather their delicate shadows up, 'swift as dreams,' at the end of their flight into the clefts, platforms, and ledges of harbourless rocks facing the North Sea. They subside by degrees, with lessening and shortening volleys of wings and cries until there comes the general shadow of night.

All shadows cease at that approach. It is the gentlest of all shades, and all others close with it. The flutters of those pulses rest. And the only visible shadowless flight is the flight of bats. The evening is the shadow of another flight. All the birds have traced wild and innumerable paths across the mid-May earth; their shadows have fled all day faster than her streams, and have overtaken all the movement of her wingless creatures. But now it is the flight of the very earth that hides the sun.

The figure and the shadow have a companion, a third, a visiting creature who leaps from the mirror to the stream, is scattered and shattered by a ripple, turned to the most inventive burlesque by the minute distortions of a Neapolitan looking-glass, and restored to decorous precision and robbed of all its separate character and spirit by the perfect plate-glass of London.

It has not been said, apparently, that even the man who sold his shadow forfeited his reflection. And the reflection would be a far more dangerous thing to have astray and at large, more compromising. For if a reflection has and obeys any laws at all, they are not easy to find. Artists will tell you how you may do almost anything else by rule, but a reflection must be done from sight. It will insist upon having its painter out of doors, and upon putting him to the touch. A boat's wake on a smooth water will be so played with by its reflection as to disappoint conjecture and to delight the eye, which is a summary way of teaching the painter simplicity and vigilance. Its design is baffling at once and inevitable, and it does not show you why. The reflection is a flash, but its production is intricate. It cares not to be understood, but is quick to be seen. A child who has 'done' a sum right, and holds the total, is not more innocent of the reasons of the way he and the figures have gone together than a landscape painter, who has captured a reflection, is ignorant of the reasons of that manifestation. The broken and sprinkled image of an oar, lasting for a moment, is as difficult a sign as the constellation designed and composed by intricate laws of stellar perspective out of alien stars. It is the prettiest trick of reflection, this fracture and dismemberment, to be so smoothly repaired when the wave is still. A shred of the image of a flying wing of a sail is carried far upon another wing—the wing of the ripple, flight to flight.

The water distributes it, mingles it, turn by turn, with shreds and patches, curves and ribbons, of the reflected sky; tosses and catches it to the utmost. The image, so interrupted, goes far, and all the interruptions are reflections of the sky.

We have not so many distinctions and definitions in our language that we can well be careless of those we have. Yet Wordsworth did something to confuse a very simple matter, with his 'swan and shadow'. There are waters, indeed, upon which the swan casts a shadow, and a shadow full of the charm of slow rivers in fertile soil—rivers that carry the soil in their fruitful waters; but that shadow does not show the swan as floating double. Not such softly troubled waters were those of St. Mary's Lake. I think Wordsworth's swan was not shadowed, but reflected. And shadow and reflection are much unlike. The one plays no pranks, or plays them with a daily regularity, drawing the caricature that amused Cowper— drawing it so unfailingly at morning and evening whenever the sun is out, that it is no small wonder it should amuse any man of Cowper's age and experience, at least to that degree. The shadow is faithful in movement, and at tether it is steady enough to make a sundial; whereas the reflection, when it is Nature's own doing and not the upholsterer's, is subject and sensitive, tremulous and fugitive, shy and mobile on water.

Nevertheless, Wordsworth must be forgiven his 'shadow,' for he has made amends to the reflection by the best line that ever described one—

It trembled, but it never passed away.

This was in long, still weather. But let a wind come by, and the image is dispersable. No flock of wild birds is wilder, though this flock hovers within recall, and when the alarm is past closes and folds into its place again. A volley of broadcast images flies deep and wide, and is gathered back to so much clam that the little town covering the island of the Lake of Orta has the chance-growing grass on its high church belfry mirrored below.

Lovely as are the village, the high field in flower, the forest reflected in Como, in Avon, and the Thames, all these waters— long rivers and broad seas—reflect nothing more wonderfully than a sail, except only the sun itself. A white sail at sea is more full of sun than any wind could fill it. The wind does but curve it to the utmost of its form, but the sun transforms it, so that it goes on the water a shining light. And that light the soft wave softly gives back. It gives back a greater light—the cloud's. When there is a bright cloud-shine after a storm, or towards evening of a varied, electric day, the calm sea, seen from a height of coast, is a vision of the sky. Or see the waters under heavens that are blue to the east and golden to the west, and every separate ripple has also its eastern colour and its western. Or on a common grey day, a Channel day, there is something generous and great in the universal grasp that the mobile waters have taken of the light. It is shattered to bits, it is flung wide, it is intricate with fine shadows.

The earth, finally, and her innumerable waters, and man and his innumerable windows, have for their heart of reflection the image of the sun himself. While that image burns within every stream, within every sea, within every lake, within every pool and pond of this world, the earth seems to multiply the very centre of life. She goes carrying suns. It is dazzling to think of that cargo, that treasury, those guests and sojourners, those strangers within her gates, who are but one and yet are so renewed. Of all the mental visions of the earth this is the most brilliant. Suns lurk throughout her daylight; suns in her deep places, separate, single, and fervent. All the coolness of the summer contains these suns; they are the heart in the breast of waters. They lie in the ice of the north, round and still in the equatorial ocean, and broken into sparkles and spray by quicker seas. They are caught in the fjords. The tides swing them up the coast and out again.

The towns, moreover, light themselves with suns. A thousand replies to the sunset shine in the windows of streets. Into a room looking to the west, the sunrise comes from windows across a road—a second-hand sunshine, but sweet enough to soften all the light—so hard from the unsunned quarter of a London sky—and bright enough to cast tender shadows: it is a charming secondary sunshine with a look somewhat as though it shone through water, through shallow waves on a beach. The room has spirit from the moment these visiting rays gain ingress; and they do but come from windows that see the east. This is the best use that glass fulfils; and many an ugly London guillotine sash, filled with cheap glass, and divided by dark bars, has, by reflection, an ardent centre of sun. The mere windows of towns reflect the authentic sun, the mirrors carry his fire, dimmed by not altered.

Poetry

Preludes (1875)
Poems (1893, a collection several times reprinted)
Other Poems (privately printed, 1896)
Later Poems (1902)
Poems (1913, an expanded collection often reprinted)
The Shepherdess and Other Verses (1914)
Ten Poems, privately printed (1915)
Poems on the War, privately printed (1916)
A Father of Women and Other Poems (1917)
Last Poems (1923)

Prose

The Rhythm of Life and Other Essays (1893)
The Colour of Life and Other Essays on Things Seen and Heard (1896)
The Children (1897)
London Impressions (1898, pictures by William Hyde and essays by Alice Meynell)
The Spirit of Place and Other Essays (1898)
Children of the Old Masters (1903)
John Ruskin (1900)
Ceres' Runaway and Other Essays (1909)
Mary, the Mother of Jesus (1912)
Childhood (1913)
Essays (1914, a selection often reprinted)
Hearts of Controversy (1917)
The Second Person Singular and Other Essays (1921)

Posthumous Anthologies

Essays of Today and Yesterday (1926) is a choice by Wilfrid Meynell of Alice's essays on women.

Wayfaring (1928) contains mainly essays, some of them previously uncollected, with a small number of appended poems.

The Poems of Alice Meynell: Complete Edition (1923, enlarged in 1940 with further posthumous poems), is the fullest edition of her verse. The text of the present selection is based on the 1940 edition, only deviating in the case of a few questionable instances of typographical indentation or lack thereof.

Prose and Poetry: Centenary Volume (1947), ed. Frederick Page, Viola Meynell, Olivia Sowerby (née Meynell) and Francis Meynell, with an introduction by Vita Sackville-West, is a handsomely produced anthology in which the prose outweighs the verse by a ratio of about 9:1.

The Wares of Autolycus (1965), ed. P.M. Fraser, is a valuable selection of literary-critical essays not collected into any of the books published during Meynell's lifetime.

Further Biographical Reading

Viola Meynell, *Alice Meynell: A Memoir* (1929)
June Badeni, *The Slender Tree: A Life of Alice Meynell* (1981)
The Selected Letters of Alice Meynell, ed. Damian Atkinson (2013)

NOTES ON THE TEXT

I began with the intention of taking as my copy-text the latest version of each poem or essay, honouring all of the author's revisions. In editing the poems I was able to hold to this course without regrets. Turning to the essays, however, the principle could not be so contentedly followed. A reviser of prose is much freer than a reviser of short metrical poems, and when Meynell, in choosing selections for her volume *Essays* (1914), revisited pieces that had been previously collected she made considerable excisions. Some of these I cannot help but regret. Further, whereas posthumous additions to her *Collected Poems* were of texts either previously unpublished or printed earlier in only a single version, this is not true of the essays: two anthologies of her essays were published in the decade after her death, *Wayfarings* and *Essays of Today and Yesterday*, both claiming in general to incorporate previously unpublished authorial revisions. Yet in the latter-named volume there is also an explicit acknowledgement that the editor, Wilfrid Meynell, had in some places made editorial interventions of his own—in keeping, he believes, with what would have been his late wife's wishes. I have felt free in the difficult cases to choose what seemed to me the best version.

In sequencing I have again adopted two different systems, one for verse and one for prose. In this I have a precedent in Meynell's own practice, since the successive editions of her verse preserved a rough sense of chronology and development, while her volume of *Essays*, also several times reissued, has its contents divided into thematic sections with no regard for chronology. Partly, no doubt, this is influenced by a traditional tendency to emphasise the 'growth of a poet', not so often or readily applied to the essayist. Yet in Meynell's work there are intrinsic reasons why the conventional approach seems appropriate. In the first place, some of her best and most famous poems were written and published much earlier than the large proportion of the rest of her work, and for me it is hard not to feel that these youthful poems, even with their later revisions, belong together and to a phase in her life. Her essays, in comparison, which were always diverse in character and occasion, show less marked signs of consistent development over time. Secondly, although one might expect the essays to be more 'topical' or 'occasional' than the poems, in fact this is not the case. It should be acknowledged, however, that in my selection of essays I have, like Meynell's original volumes, focused on pieces of a generally 'essayistic' or belletrist kind, and have not included any of the more directly topical articles that Meynell contributed to magazines and newspapers. To have included many of these would probably have made a different method desirable. (Given my constraints of space, and with a similar effect, I have also left out such pieces of sustained and specific literary criticism as were written as reviews or prefaces, or upon a writer's death.)

The poems, then, I have kept in roughly chronological order, grouping together the contents of each volume or pamphlet. Uncollected or posthumously published poems are inserted according to the date either of their first publication or, in the case of the juvenilia, of their composition. The dates of first publication in book form (or elsewhere in the case of posthumously collected pieces) are therefore clear from the Table of Contents, though the text is based throughout, except for a few instances of anomalous or doubtful indentations, on the 1923/40 *Complete Edition* of the poems, which incorporates the author's revisions in prior collections. I have not thought it necessary or desirable, given that this is a selection only, to retain the ordering of poems found in the original volumes.

The essays are arranged freely and the sources for these are as follows.—

'The Rhythm of Life'. Text from *Essays*. Earlier collected in *Rhythm of Life*.

'A Woman in Grey'. Text from *Colour of Life*.

'Prue'. Text from *Essays*.

'Mrs. Johnson'. Text from *Essays*.

'Victorian Caricature'. Text from *Essays*. Earlier collected, as 'Penultimate Caricature', in *Rhythm of Life*.

'The Lady of the Lyrics'. Text from *Spirit of Place*, not the later version, shortened by the author or possibly Wilfrid Meynell, in *Essays of Today and Yesterday*.

'Composure'. Text from *Essays*. Earlier collected in *Rhythm of Life*.

'Rejection'. Text from *Rhythm of Life*.

'The Point of Honour'. Text from *Essays*. Earlier collected in *Rhythm of Life*.

'Pocket Vocabularies'. Text from *Rhythm of Life*.

'The Hours of Sleep'. Text from *Essays*. Earlier collected in *Spirit of Place*.

'Solitude'. Text from *Essays*, not the revised and heavily pruned version, entitled 'Solitudes', later collected in *Wayfaring*. Earlier collected (as 'Solitudes') in *Spirit of Place*.

'Nooks'. Text from *Wayfaring*.

'Near the Ground'. Text from *Childhood*.

'The Child of Tumult'. Text from *Essays*. Earlier collected in *Ceres' Runaway*.

'The Child of Subsiding Tumult'. Text from *Essays*. Earlier collected in *Ceres' Runaway*.

'The Horizon'. Text from *Essays*. Earlier collected in *Spirit of Place*.

'Cloud'. Text from *Colour Of Life*, not the later,
    abbreviated version in *Essays*.
'Shadows'. Text from *Wayfaring*. Earlier collected in
    Spirit of Place and *Essays*.
'Reflections'. Text from *Wayfaring*.

For the sake of consistency I have removed the speech marks
enclosing inset quotations in some of the copytexts.

ACKNOWLEDGEMENTS

To Alice Meynell's great-grandson, Oliver Hawkins, as literary executor, and to other members of the family descended from the Meynells, I am grateful both for their hospitality at Greatham on the occasion of a symposium marking the centenary of Alice Meynell's death, and for permission to quote from manuscript and other materials remaining in copyright. Oliver has also generously helped in the search for a cover image. Thanks to Sarah Parker, too, for organising the 2022 centenary event, and indeed to all the other participants for inspiration and shared enthusiasm. For helpful conversations and general advice I would like to thank Sarah Green and Alison Hennegan, and I would not forget the various students with whom I have discussed some of these texts over the last few years, including those who bravely faced the intellectual complexities of a Meynell poem in the course of their admissions interviews.

Finally, I am of course most grateful to Laura Mulvey, another of Alice Meynell's great-grandchildren, for her Preface, her suggestions on the sequencing of essays, and the stimulating discussions along the way. Among other things, her emphasis on the maternal influence vividly and valuably counterbalances the more usual stress on Meynell's debt to her father and his scrupulous, exacting intellectualism. Taken together with the Lacanian thinking that Laura's Preface also evokes, and the idea of *écriture feminine*, this seems to open up very suggestively a new way of looking at the creative tension of 'wildness' and 'law' that I have drawn out in my Introduction. Meanwhile, having myself gravitated disproportionately towards the poems in my remarks, I am glad that the Preface, with its focus on Meynell's essayistic prose, which was after all her most frequent medium, corrects this leaning too.

AW